W9-AQZ-928

WHAT PEOPLE ARE SAYING ABOUT

Leadership from the Inside Out . . .

"Some books are noteworthy in and of themselves. Others serve as signs that something important is happening in the world. Kevin Cashman's *Leadership from the Inside Out* meets both criteria. Throw in the fact that it is well-designed for reading and for doing the exercises provided throughout, and you have a real mind-opener."

—Perry Pascarella, contributing editor, *American Management Review,*
former editor-in-chief, *Industry Week,* and author of *Leveraging People and Profit*

"*Leadership from the Inside Out* is a major paradigm shift in leadership development. It gives you the tools to go directly to the heart of all significant leadership transformation: growing as a person to grow as a leader."

—Paul Walsh, Chairman & CEO, The Pillsbury Company

"Sooner or later, every leader who would like to lead more effectively finds himself blocked. Kevin Cashman's book illuminates how we can find the means within ourselves to identify and remove these barriers in order to fulfill our leadership destiny."

—J. P. Donlon, Editor, *Chief Executive* magazine

"With hundreds of books to choose from on the topic of leadership, it is unusual to come across one, *Leadership from the Inside Out*, that has the potential to make a meaningful change in your life."

—Larry Perlman, Chairman & CEO, Ceridian Corporation

"To be recognized as a leader, one must embrace moral values, professional skills, and character qualities that create an environment in which people want to perform at their best. *Leadership from the Inside Out* is a practical and inspirational resource guide that addresses the skills and qualities needed for congruent leadership."

—Angeles Arrien, Ph.D., cultural anthropologist and author of
The Four-Fold Way and *Signs of Life*

"*Leadership from the Inside Out* serves as an important wake-up call for those who are ready to unleash the power of authentic leadership."

—Ken Melrose, Chairman & CEO, The Toro Company, and author of
Making the Grass Greener on Your Side: A CEO's Journey to Leading by Serving

"External forces are often antithetical to superior leadership. This book, *Leadership from the Inside Out,* keeps the reader on track by outlining the personal practices and spiritual principles that are essential for leaders facing the challenges of the 21st century. All executives should read it for encouragement and success!"

—Jim Secord, CEO, Lakewood Publications,
and Publisher, *Training Magazine*

"Authenticity is the single most important quality of leadership. In *Leadership from the Inside Out*, Cashman not only captures the essence of inner-driven, intentional leadership, he gives both seasoned and emerging leaders a road map to navigate the challenges of personal and professional growth."

—Bob Kidder, CEO, Borden, and former CEO, Duracell

"*Leadership from the Inside Out* honors 'mastery of' life and enterprise rather than 'mastery over' others and circumstances. Cashman's advocacy of intrinsic dominion over traditional extrinsic domination is sorely needed if we are to transcend the prevailing crisis in leadership."

—John E. Renesch, Editor, *The New Leader* newsletter

"Reading *Leadership from the Inside Out* is like going on your own executive retreat. Kevin Cashman takes you on an in-depth journey that helps you to reflect on your life, challenge your thinking, practice new ways of being, and ultimately experience transformative growth from the inside out."

—James Ericson, Co-founder, The Masters Forum

"Leadership arising from character flows through the heart and spirit of people from the inside out. Cashman invites us to be a part of this 'flow,' asking the important questions about our inner resources of character so that our actions originate from our true essence."

—Gay Hendricks, Ph.D., Co-founder, Foundation for Twenty-First
Century Leadership, and co-author of *The Corporate Mystic*

"This book is a must-read for those seeking to be a redeeming force in the environment, work, and home that surrounds them."

—Bob Griffin, President, Pacing Business, Medtronic, Inc.

"Today's organizations require authentic leaders who are able to foster participation and creativity at every level. *Leadership from the Inside Out* is an excellent guide for those who want to replace the old command-and-control model with true strategic leadership."

—Marilyn W. Norris, Editor, *Strategy & Leadership* magazine

"*Leadership from the Inside Out* is both profound and practical, a rare mix in our time. This book shows how it is possible to understand and transform leadership at the core level, through the stories of people who have succeeded. Leadership requires presence; this book encourages our presence in life."

—Stephen Rechtschaffen, M.D., President, Omega Institute,
and author of *Time Shifting*

"*Leadership from the Inside Out* is a resource that spans the ages, integrates multiple disciplines, has experiential validity, and includes proven practical applications. Using (not just reading) this book is a transformative, peak experience."

—Robert Hayles, Ph.D., 1996 Chairman of the Board, American Society
for Training & Development, and co-author of *The Diversity Directive*

"Cashman gets it just right: Leadership really does come from the inside out. His book covers the internal bases that leaders too often neglect—authenticity, purpose, and self-knowledge."

—Lee Bolman, Ph.D., author of *Leading with Soul: An Uncommon Journey of Spirit* and *Reframing Organizations*

"In *Leadership from the Inside Out*, Cashman provides us with the tools to develop the inner strength necessary to cope with great change, let go of limiting beliefs and behaviors, and attain leadership potential."

—Larry Wilson, Founder and Vice Chairman, Pecos River Division— Aon Consulting, Inc., and co-author of *Stop Selling, Start Partnering*

"Kevin Cashman is a renaissance man of our time. His personal mastery is mirrored by a successful business that has guided thousands of people to live more fulfilling, masterful lives. Now he has articulated his experience and wisdom through *Leadership from the Inside Out*. This is an important book written by an authentic leader!"

—Craig and Patricia Neal, Founders, The Heartland Institute

"This is an incredibly useful book for all leaders committed to the personal journey which supports high performance. Cashman invites us to explore ourselves and our influence on others so as to bring forth genuine leadership."

—Don Goldfus, Chairman & CEO, Apogee Enterprises, Inc.

"I highly recommend this book. Cashman's principles of authenticity, self-expression, and creating value make *Leadership from the Inside Out* a profound self-mastery tool for leaders at all levels."

—Al Schuman, President & CEO, Ecolab, Inc.

"*Leadership from the Inside Out* is the perfect book for today's overworked and overwhelmed executive. Delving into it a bit at a time will, almost without your realizing it, help you find the time to use Cashman's tools for realizing your full potential."

—Beverly Goldberg, co-author of *Corporation on a Tightrope* and *Dynamic Planning*

"Cashman is a truth-teller. As a leader, if you want more authenticity and commitment in your life, buy this book . . . then read it and do it."

—David Prosser, Chairman, RTW, Inc.

"*Leadership from the Inside Out* is a heart-provoking leadership journey that transcends intellect and penetrates one's essence. Cashman's genuine call for awakening is crucial to leaders at all levels of organizations."

—Tom Gegax, Head Coach, Tires Plus Groupe, Ltd.

"True adventure always involves the exploration of one's innermost spirit. *Leadership from the Inside Out* is a compass that helps you navigate this hidden domain as a means to bring out full leadership capacity with honesty and renewed energy."

—Ann Bancroft, polar explorer (first woman to reach North and South
Poles) and Director, American Women's Expedition Foundation

"*Leadership from the Inside Out* touches the heart and soul of transformative leadership. Practicing the seven pathways of leadership will lead us into the next century with courage, meaning, and purpose."

—Bill DeFoore, Ph.D., co-editor of *The New Bottom Line* and
Rediscovering the Soul of Business: A Renaissance of Values

"Outstanding! *Leadership from the Inside Out* is a must-read for anyone serious about making positive change in their lives and in the world."

—Robert Hawthorne, CEO, Select Comfort Corporation, and former
President, The Pillsbury Company

"Serving as bedrock for this valuable book are Kevin's powerful, intimate experiences with people as they challenge themselves to grow into their leadership potential. His capacity to synthesize experience into principles and practices, integrated with his ability to tell stories richly yet succinctly—to combine insight and illustration—again and again adds up to wisdom.

—Barbara Shipka, author of *Leadership in a Challenging
World: A Sacred Journey*

"Leadership begins with truth and consummates itself in trust. *Leadership from the Inside Out* gives you some very practical ways to live these crucial principles. The support found in these principles surmounts the challenges we must deal with as we approach the next century."

—Robert James, President, Allianz of North America

"In his new book, *Leadership from the Inside Out*, Kevin Cashman joins the great philosophers of history in maintaining that we must build internal foundations for the greatest external results. He offers practical wisdom and guidance for leaders who want to increase personal effectiveness in the most enduring and satisfying way."

—Tom Morris, Ph.D., Chairman, Morris Institute for Human Values,
and author of *True Success: A New Philosophy of Excellence*, and *If Aristotle
Ran General Motors: The New Soul of Business*

"If you want personal transformation, then buy *Leadership from the Inside Out*. It will guide you through the unexplored territories we often miss in our frenetic-paced business world."

—Trudy Rautio, Executive Vice President and CFO, Carlson Hospitality Worldwide

"Our knowledge of leadership has soared in the past few years, far beyond tactics and concepts, into the powerful but elusive realm of human spirit. Here, finally, is a book that not only explains what this means, but also shows us step-by-step how to get there!"

—Jack Hawley, author of *Reawakening the Spirit in Work: The Power of
Dharmic Management*

LEADERSHIP
FROM THE INSIDE OUT

Becoming a Leader for Life

KEVIN CASHMAN

TCLG, llc
LeaderSource
One Financial Plaza
120 South 6ᵗʰ Street
Suite 2600
Minneapolis, MN 55402
phone: (612) 375-9277
fax: (612) 334-5727
e-mail: Info@LeaderSource.com
web: www.leadersource.com

First edition.

Printed in the United States of America
10 9   08 07 06 05

ISBN: 0-9752765-0-6

Leadership from the Inside Out is a registered service mark of Kevin Cashman. Executive to Leader Institute, LeaderCatalyst, LeaderSynergy, NewLeader, Integrated Manager, and The Self-Managed Career are all registered service marks of LeaderSource Limited.

Cover photo by Peggy Lauritsen
Author photos by David Neiman (inside) and John Noltner (jacket)
Cover design by Peggy Lauritsen Design Group

This book is dedicated to those rare leaders who have the courage to commit to authentic personal transformation in order to enrich the world around them.

ACKNOWLEDGMENTS

Writing a book is definitely an odyssey in personal growth. It has become apparent to me that writing is less about proclaiming what you know and more about being open to the learning coming your way. I am very grateful for all the learning that has come my way through so many great people over the years. The further I venture down my life journey, the more painfully aware I become of *how little* I really know and *how much* others have taught me. I feel very fortunate to be associated with so many growing, gifted human beings.

My warmest, most heartfelt thanks to all the wonderful people at LeaderSource. I am blessed to be with such a brilliant, caring group of people. Special gratitude to Cecile Burzynski, Janet Feldman, Sherri Rogalski, Faye Way, Lynne Way, Katie Cooney, David Brings, Bill McCarthy, Joe Eastman, Jody Thone Lande, Ed Anderson, Anne Tessien, and Robert Riskin for all your help, learning, and support in the preparation of this book. Thanks also to Sidney Reisberg, who has retired from LeaderSource but whose mentorship lives on.

Thanks to the hundreds of clients I have been fortunate enough to serve over the past 20 years. Your gratitude and support over the years have been tremendous. I wish I could name all of you but that would fill up an entire book— thanks for the privilege to know and to serve all of you.

Thanks to the 50+ CEOs who shared their thoughts, feelings, and life experiences with me as I prepared the book. Our lively exchanges were helpful, provocative, and insightful. It's a shame CEOs don't take more time to talk about the essence of what they do—thanks for taking the time to do so. Special thanks to Paul Walsh, Ken Melrose, Gus Blanchard, Larry Perlman, Jim Secord, David Prosser, John Hetterick, Al Schuman, Bob Kidder, Rob Hawthorne, Robert James, Tom Votel, Bill George, Mac Lewis, John Sundet, and Tom Gegax for their generous sharing.

Thanks to Ken Shelton, Trent Price, Robert Chapman, and the entire Executive Excellence team. After a long journey together, we actually brought this book to life! Your persistence and enthusiasm are greatly appreciated.

Thanks to Margie Adler for her editing gifts—we actually had fun, didn't we? Thanks to Peggy Lauritsen and her design team for the beautiful cover design—didn't they do a great job? Thanks to Fred and Sarah Bell Haberman for their excellent public relations efforts—your excitement and belief in this book always give me a lift. Thanks to writer-author Jack Forem for his encouragement and friendship—the moment you told me that I was a "really good writer" sustained me through a couple of years of drafts. Thanks to James Flaherty for being a "coaches coach" and sharing wisdom with our team.

Special thanks to Bob Silverstein for rejecting my initial manuscript and then sharing with me that I needed to "find my voice." Although I was devastated at first, it was the best feedback I received—it literally transformed my entire approach to writing.

My deepest thanks to Denise—your support, appreciation, and friendship are a constant source of both practical wisdom and soulful connection. Like the day when we were exploring the age-old question, "Is the nature of humankind good or evil?" and you thoughtfully reflected, "The nature of humankind is." I'm still pondering that one!

My most important thank you goes to you, the reader. I wrote this book for people like you—leaders interested in personal growth and transformation. Thanks for the opportunity to share and to grow with you.

TABLE OF CONTENTS

The Search for Something More
Don't Place "Descartes" Before "the Source"
Techniques to Unfold Being
Reflection on Being Mastery: Exploring the Leader Within
Connecting with Our Inner Self
Being and Executive Presence
Leadership Benefits of Being
Leadership Growth Commitments for Being Mastery
Four Points of Awareness for Leading from Being
Being Mastery Summary

PATHWAY SIX: BALANCE MASTERY

Challenges of Balance for Executives
What Happened to the Life of Leisure?
Balance: No Longer a Luxury, a Matter of Survival for Leaders
What Healthy, Productive 100-Year-Olds Can Teach Leaders
Balance Is a Dynamic Process
The Ten Signs of Balance Mastery
The Ten Signs of Imbalance
Nature's Balancing Act: Rest and Activity
The Ten Balance Points of Leaders
Reflection on Leading by Centering Our Life
Leadership Growth Commitments for Balance Mastery
Balance Mastery Summary

PATHWAY SEVEN: ACTION MASTERY

Going Beyond Our Limits
Earning a Living or Feeding a Community?
Three Core Principles Underlying Action Mastery
The Two Steps to Action Mastery
Leadership from the Inside Out Journal
Seven Points of Awareness for Leading as a Whole Person
Parting Thoughts for Your Journey Ahead

HOW TO USE THIS BOOK

. . . from the Inside Out

Leadership from the Inside Out is a "wake-up call" to remind us that our ability to grow as a leader is based on our ability to grow as a person. We will not analyze the *external act* of leadership into a formula of "ten easy-to-follow" quick tips. Rather, we will take a reflective journey to foster the personal awakening needed to enhance our leadership effectiveness.

You need not rush. As a matter of fact, I encourage you to set aside the urge to plough through the pages. When a thought or feeling surfaces, close the book, put up your feet, and explore the insight. If you want to capture a key insight, jot it down in the space provided. Instead of just reading the book, experience it, digest it, and integrate it into your life.

You've probably read all sorts of personal and professional development books before; treat this one differently. Savor it as you would a walk with an old friend on a calm, sunny afternoon. There is no need to hurry, to anticipate, or to reach the end of your journey. Enjoy the experience itself.

On days you feel like taking a short walk, just skim through the quotes. You'll find one or two that speak to your needs that day.

If you are ready to begin, let's walk together down the pathways to mastery of *Leadership from the Inside Out*.

The Beginning
of the Journey

It is a magical night: one of those rare December evenings when the cold and the warmth mix just right to blanket everything with big, fluffy, crystalline flakes of snow. As the snow deepens so does the silence in the atmosphere. I could be sitting in a log cabin in Vail, but I'm not. I'm in a traffic jam on a Minneapolis freeway—and enjoying every minute of it! Being in a car at rush hour can be either a prison or a monastic retreat. It all depends on your perspective.

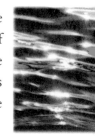

Everything looks so perfect. Everything feels so silent. Does it really matter that I'm going to be late? Even though I probably should feel stressed by this situation, instead I welcome the opportunity to reflect. As I sink into a meditative state, I begin to think about my day. And what a day it was—a rich mixture of purpose, passion, emotion, and concentrated learning.

Our coaching team had just finished guiding a senior executive of a major company through our *Executive to Leader Institute*. It was an intensive, rewarding three days. Our team of coaches helped the client master a career-life-leadership plan by integrating a comprehensive look at his professional and personal life. In a way we helped him to observe himself just as I was observing the snowfall—clearly, objectively, and appreciatively. At the end of the last session he had said, "You know, I've been through all sorts of assessments and development programs. But this is the first time things have really made sense to me. I've gotten pieces of the puzzle before, but never the whole picture. I clearly understand where I'm at, where I'm headed, and what I need to do to really enhance my effectiveness. What would my organization be like if everyone mastered the same sense of personal conviction and clarity I have now?"

As the snow piles up, I'm feeling very fortunate. Playing a role in helping people awaken their potential is a deeply fulfilling thing to do. To help people connect to their purposeful potential occasionally would be fortunate. But to coach thousands of managers and executives for nearly 20 years is truly rewarding. I'm feeling very blessed, when suddenly I snap out of my thoughtful state and catch a glimpse of the clock. I'm an hour late! When the heck is this snow going to let up!

Give me beauty in the inward soul; may the outward and inward man be at one.

—Socrates

My good fortune goes beyond playing a role in the growth and development of leaders. I've been truly fortunate to have learned a great deal along the way. I've gained insight into the human dynamics supporting mastery, success, fulfillment, and effectiveness. I've learned also that these principles are not reserved for a few exceptional leaders. They are fundamental insights available to guide and to inspire all of us.

While reading this book you may think, "Is this book about leadership, or is it about personal development?" It's about both. As much as we try to separate the leader from the person, the two are totally inseparable. Unfortunately, many people tend to split off the *act of leadership* from the person. We tend to view leadership as an external event. We see it only as something people do. The view of this book is different. Leadership is not simply something we do. It comes from somewhere inside us. Leadership is a process, an intimate expression of who we are. It is our being in action. Our being, our personhood, says as much about us as a leader as the act of leading itself. Paul Walsh, Chairman and CEO of Pillsbury, recently told me, "The missing link in leadership development is growing the person to grow the leader." As we grow, so shall we lead.

We lead by virtue of who we are. Some people reading this book will make breakthroughs and then lead their own lives more effectively. Others will develop themselves and passionately lead major organizations to new heights. Whether we are at an early stage in our career, a knowledge worker or a corporate executive, we are all CEOs of our own lives. The only difference is the domain of influence. The process is the same; we lead from who we are. The leader and the person are one. As we learn to master our growth as a person, we will be on the path to mastery of *Leadership from the Inside Out*.

What does *mastery* of leadership mean to you? To many people it is mastery *of* something: mastery *of* the skill to be a dynamic public speaker, mastery *of* strategic planning and visioning, mastery *of* consistent achievements and results. Instead of being seen as an ongoing, internal growth process, mastery is usually seen as mastery *of* something outside of ourselves. When you think about it, it's no wonder that our ideas about mastery and leadership tend to be externalized. Our training, development, and educational systems focus on learning about *things*. We learn *what* to think, not *how* to think. We learn *what* to do, not *how* to be. We learn *what* to achieve, not *how* to achieve. We learn about *things*, not the *nature of things*. We tend to fill up the container of knowledge but rarely consider comprehending it, expanding it, or using it more effectively.

INSIGHTS • REFLECTIONS • COMMITMENTS •

In organizations, this external pattern continues. As leaders of organizations and communities, we receive recognition for our external mastery. Our success is measured by the degree to which we have mastered our external environment. Revenue, profit, new product breakthroughs, cost savings, and market share are only some of the measures of our external competencies. Few would question the value of achieving and measuring external results. That isn't the real issue. The core questions are: Where do the external results come from? Is focusing on external achievement the sole source of greater accomplishment? Could it be that our single-minded focus on external results is causing us to miss the underlying dynamics supporting peak performance?

Our definitions of leadership also tend to be externalized. Most descriptions of leadership focus on the *outer manifestations* of leadership (i.e., vision, judgment, creativity, charisma, drive, etc.), instead of getting to the *essence of leadership* itself. What is the essence of leadership? After 20 years of wrestling with this question, I've come to this simple yet profound realization: **Leadership is authentic self-expression that creates value**. The implications of this definition are quite far-reaching. From this new perspective, leadership is not seen as hierarchical—it exists everywhere in organizations. The roles of leadership change, but the core process is the same. Anyone who is authentically self-expressing and creating value is leading. Some may self-express and create value through ideas, others through systems, others through people, but the essence is the same.

> *Anyone can lead, and there is no single chief executive officer. There is a problem of getting used to the idea of no single chief, but the passage of time will allay that.*
>
> —Robert Greenleaf

Reacting to this definition of leadership, John Hetterick, former President of Tonka and CEO of Rollerblade, told me, "This definition of leadership speaks to me. The single biggest issue organizations face is inspiring leadership at all levels."

Using this definition, we acknowledge that there are an infinite number of ways to manifest leadership. There are as many styles of leadership as there are leaders. Viewing leadership from this vantage point, we will be exploring three essential questions to enhance our leadership effectiveness:

- How *authentic* are we as a leader?
- How deep and broad is our *self-expression*?
- How much *value* are we creating?

Leadership from the Inside Out is about our ongoing journey to unfold and to express our purposeful inner life to make a more positive impact on the world around us. Bill George, Chairman and CEO of Medtronic, shares this view: "As leaders, the more we can unleash our whole capabilities—mind, body, spirit—the more value we can create within and outside of our organizations." Mastery of *Leadership from the Inside Out* is not merely a function of achieving things. It is principally about achieving one thing—consciously making a difference from within.

The purpose of this book is to guide you down seven pathways to the mastery of leadership from within. I will do this by sharing our* distilled insights from working with hundreds of leaders. Although the subsequent chapters will elaborate, there are a few essential themes which consistently surface as we help people to master their leadership effectiveness:

INSIGHTS • REFLECTIONS
• COMMITMENTS •

- As the person grows, the leader grows. The missing element in most leadership development programs is growing the person to grow the leader.

- Most definitions of leadership need to be turned inside out, moving from viewing leadership only in terms of its external manifestations to seeing it from its internal source.

- Helping leaders to connect with their essence, their character, is central to effective executive development.

* Since the work we do at LeaderSource and the *Executive to Leader Institute* involves integrated teams of coaches working together to impact individual and organizational effectiveness, I cannot accurately write about the work without saying "our," "we," and so forth.

- Leaders who learn to bring their purpose to conscious awareness experience dramatic, quantum increases in energy, effectiveness, and fulfillment.

- Leaders who integrate personal power and results power with synergy power accelerate their leadership effectiveness.

- Leaders who work on achieving career-life balance are not only healthier, but more effective.

The essence of leadership is not giving things or even providing visions. It is offering oneself and one's spirit.

—Lee Bolman and Terrence Deal

- Transforming leadership development programs from a series of fragmented, content-driven events to an integrated, inside-out growth process greatly enhances personal, professional, and organizational excellence.

Leadership from the Inside Out involves awakening our inner identity, purpose, and vision so that our lives thereafter are dedicated to a conscious, intentional manner of living. This inner mastery focuses our diverse intentions and aspirations into a purposeful flow where increased effectiveness is a natural result.

As we move to a more fulfilled manner of living, a focus on purpose replaces our single-minded focus on external success. However, our purpose cannot stay "bottled up" inside; we must express it. This purposeful intention and action serves as the energetic, inspired basis for enhanced leadership effectiveness and achievement. Unfortunately, I've lost track of the number of times I've met with a CEO, business owner, or corporate executive who had lost connection to this inner core of success.

John, a business owner, approached me a while ago. By all external measures he was a great success. He had a thriving business. He recently built a new facility to house his expanding operations. But something was missing. When he sat down with me, he opened up immediately by saying, "You know, everyone thinks I'm a big success. My neighbors think I'm successful. Even my friends think I'm successful. My family thinks I'm successful. But you know what? I'm miserable. I'm unhappy in what I'm doing. My whole life I've been just *successfully reacting to circumstances*. I got my degree and that defined my first job, and that first job defined my second job, and so on. And before I knew it I had this business, a family, and a mortgage. Recently I 'woke up' and said to myself, 'Is this me? Is this my life, or just a series of circumstances I've successfully reacted to?' I'm not sure what to do, but I have this deep sense that I need to take my life back."

From a development perspective, many leaders of organizations today are like John. They are like naturally gifted athletes who have mastered their external performance capabilities but have neglected the inner dynamics supporting their success and fulfillment. What happens to natural athletes who become coaches? They usually have an extremely difficult and frustrating time. Why? Most often it is because these people have not comprehended from the inside out how they became great. As a result, it is challenging to mentor others to greatness, and it is equally challenging to be consciously aware of how to replicate their own success in the future. This is why all significant growth and development begins with self-leadership, mastery of oneself.

INSIGHTS • REFLECTIONS • COMMITMENTS •

When we define our identity and purpose only in terms of external results, the circumstances of our lives define us. In this externally driven state of identity, life is fragile, vulnerable, and at risk. Everything that happens to us defines who we are. We are success. We are failure. We become our circumstances. Life defines us. Our core identity and passionate purpose are overshadowed by the events of our lives. Success may even be present, but mastery has escaped us. Unintentionally, we have chosen to "major" in the minor things of life. Can we lead when we can't see beyond the external circumstances surrounding us?

Bill, a senior executive in a large company, was caught in this external trap, but he didn't know it. His career had been a fast and consistent ascent to the top. He had the "right degree," his background was with the "right companies," his results were always outstanding. However, his single-minded pursuit of success had great costs. Without intending to, he left a wide wake of people in his path to success, and as a

Awakening leading to transformation versus process leading to change.

—Zen Proverb

result, had few close supporters. At earlier stages in his career, this was not an issue. As he advanced, it became an increasing problem. One day his boss approached him and said, "Bill, your results are outstanding, but we need more than that. The way you're getting results is starting to diminish your effectiveness here." Bill was shocked. A flood of thoughts came to mind: "What do you mean my results are not enough?" "Since when has my style been an issue?" "Am I missing something here?" Bill's externally built facade of success was being questioned by his boss *and* by himself. This jolt was exactly what he needed to foster his development to the next level.

After a few days, Bill arrived in my office for leadership coaching. The shock of his boss's comments and his need to reconcile them with his limited self-understanding had put him in a reflective mood. "I've been avoiding this. If I'm honest with myself I know I have to do some work—not the type of work I'm accustomed to: work on me. But I'm totally at a loss. My whole life has been focused on achieving: getting the grades in school, winning in sports, getting results in business. When I'm faced with how to grow as a person, I'm lost. I'm even beginning to wonder what's really important to me anymore. My life has been invested in getting results. Now that's not enough. What do I do?"

After a couple of months of intensive work, Bill literally turned his life inside out. He started to lead from his core values. He built relationships with people. He mastered the power of inner-driven, purposeful leadership. His environment responded to his newfound sense of self. His boss, co-workers, friends, and family all felt that something significant, something of real substance, had happened.

It's important to note that we didn't try to change Bill or even Bill's behavior by taking him through some sort of "charm school." We helped him wake up.

He woke up to his identity. He woke up to his values and purpose. He woke up to his vision. This inside-out mastery authentically reconnected him to himself. It was there all the time, but he needed to awaken it. Like Bill, many of us are in a slumber. Rarely questioning where we are going and why, we go about our business and relationships day after day. Unfortunately, it often takes a traumatic event—a death, a termination, a divorce, a disease, or a crisis—to bring us out of the depths of our slumber. But why wait for a shocking awakening? Why not choose to wake up gently now?

INSIGHTS • REFLECTIONS • COMMITMENTS •

REFLECTION

AWAKENING

Go to your favorite spot to sit. Get comfortable. Close your eyes but
don't lie down. (Remember, this is an awakening exercise, so our goal is
to wake up, not to sleep!) Listen to your internal dialogue and chatter:
"This is a dumb exercise!" "Why did I buy this book?" "I'm hungry."
"I'm tired." "I'm worried about . . ." Observe the dialogue in a non-
judging way. Don't mind your thoughts and feelings; just let them be
there and pass in and out. Let your thoughts settle down. This will happen naturally in your non-judging state.

Start to listen. Listen for your inner voice, not the one in your head with the
dialogue and thoughts. Listen for the one in the center of your chest, the
"voice" that speaks to you through feelings, inspirations, and intuitions.

From that place, ask questions and listen: "What is really important to
me? How do I really want to live my life? What gives passion, meaning,
and purpose to my life? How can I make even more of a difference? How
can I live connected to these inner values?" Let the questions and
answers come to you easily and spontaneously.

Some people prefer doing this while listening to gentle music, others while
walking; there are many ways to open up to this state. Use whatever way
works for you and practice it regularly. There are endless layers to awaken.
If you're a bit uncomfortable or embarrassed at first, don't worry about it.
Over time you will settle into it, and your discomfort will pass.

When was the last time you woke up in the morning feeling thankful, fulfilled, and happy to be alive? On these days, the sun seemed brighter, your sense of self stronger, your life's purpose clearer, and your mental and physical energies more abundant. These experiences did not happen by accident. Several aspects of your life "came together." Your self-appreciation, relationships, career, health, and lifestyle were all "more alive" at these times. As a result, you found yourself thinking, feeling, leading, and achieving in a more positive and fulfilling way.

INSIGHTS • REFLECTIONS • COMMITMENTS •

For at least a brief period of time, each of us experiences these masterful moments. How can we experience them on a more consistent basis? Unfortunately there is not a simple answer. There are no quick-fix programs in leadership development. Programs that take shortcuts may get some immediate results by temporarily masking acute symptoms, but the chronic situation remains. Over time, the person returns to an even more difficult condition. "Quick fixes" may be quick, but they don't fix anything. The people I've worked with over the years are looking for something more—mastery of excellence over the long haul.

These people are not interested in getting "psyched-up" by a motivational speaker; they are interested in substance, results, and process. They want to reach a deeper, more comprehensive level to master their lives as a whole.

Knowingly or unknowingly, we attempt to master personal and professional situations according to how we *interpret* our experiences. We filter our experiences through our unique structure of interpretation and create our personal reality. For instance, if we were in a totally dark room, we could attempt to gain mastery by interpreting it in a variety of ways:

- We could curse the darkness and become very effective at blaming it for all our problems;

- We could struggle and strain, trying with all our might to force the darkness out of the room;

> *Those who think that the world is a dark place are blind to the light that might illuminate their lives.*
>
> —Wayne Dyer

- We could accept the darkness as a natural part of our existence and even develop an entire philosophy of life around our particular dark experience;

- We could pretend the darkness did not exist and maybe even convince ourselves that the room is actually full of light;

- *Or* we could take the advice of people who have been in this room before: "Turn on the light switch and dispel the darkness."

Leadership from the Inside Out is about lighting the pathways to our growth and development. It is not about ignoring negativity, convincing ourselves it does not exist or pretending things are fine when they are not. Joseph Campbell, in *The Power of Myth,* described how effective, heroic people acknowledged and faced both the darkness and the light. They learned to acknowledge both realities as part of the whole. But, as Campbell emphasized, "Although they stand at the neutral point between darkness and light, they always leaned into the light." *Leadership from the Inside Out* is about mastering the process of leaning into the light.

After years of helping people in their career and life effectiveness, we have identified seven pathways to mastery of *Leadership from the Inside Out*. These pathways to mastery are not stages of development arranged in a sequential or hierarchical order. Rather, they are an ongoing, interrelated growth process in which the pathways constantly are illuminating one another. When arranged together, we can think of them as an integrated whole, with each path supporting progress toward a more fulfilling destination: leading more effectively from within.

Now it's time to begin our journey down the pathways for mastery of *Leadership from the Inside Out*. Each chapter that follows will give you a road map to navigate your way to a more fulfilling and effective life.

Pathway One: Personal Mastery

Leading Through Authentic Self-Expression

Personal Mastery is the ongoing commitment to unfolding and authentically expressing who we are.

I once heard this story about a priest, who was confronted by a soldier while he was walking down a road in pre-revolutionary Russia. The soldier, aiming his rifle at the priest, commanded, "Who are you? Where are you going? Why are you going there?" Unfazed, the priest calmly replied, "How much do they pay you?" Somewhat surprised, the soldier responded, "Twenty-five kopecks a month." The priest paused, and in a deeply thoughtful manner said, "I have a proposal for you. I'll pay you fifty kopecks each month if you stop me here every day and challenge me to respond to those *same three questions*."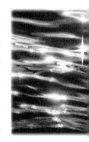

How many of us have a "soldier" confronting us with life's tough questions and pushing us to examine and to develop ourselves more thoroughly? If "character is our fate," as Heraclitus wrote, do we step back often enough both to question and to affirm ourselves in order to reveal our character? As we lead ourselves and others through tough challenges, do we draw on the inner resources of our character, or do we lose ourselves in the pressures of the situation? A recent event clarified some of these principles for me.

The Voice of Personal Mastery

I received a call on a Friday. IBM wanted a presentation for its Human Resources Group in New York. They were interested in hearing about our latest coaching program for developing leaders on all levels of the organization. Although we had done work for IBM before, we were excited because of this project's potential. Before I knew it, we were in New York, and it was the evening before our early morning presentation. Slowly but surely, my excitement turned into anxiety. Remembering the story I heard about the professional athlete who ended his Nike endorsement possibilities by walking into their headquarters with Reebok shoes on his feet, I realized that I had better not walk into IBM with my Compaq. At the last minute I switched computers for the demonstration.

I worried about the software transfer to the IBM PC: "What if there's a problem? What if I get stuck in the demonstration because I'm unfamiliar with this particular computer? Where are my overheads? Have I tailored the presentation to their needs?" The more I questioned my preparedness, the more doubtful I felt. Finally, my uncertainty culminated in my fear that, "I'm not ready for this presentation!" At this crucial moment I needed that soldier asking me, "Who are you? Where are you going? Why are you going there?" Instead, an interesting thing happened. As soon as I acknowledged my true fear, a calm washed over me, and a steady, confident inner voice affirmed, "You've been preparing for this presentation all your life. Just be yourself. Don't worry about what you're going to say or how it's going to go. Just be yourself, and it will be fine."

> *Every man must be his own leader. He now knows enough not to follow other people. He must follow the light that's within himself, and through this light he will create a new community.*
>
> —Laurens Van Der Post

The voice of Personal Mastery had spoken, so I listened. I went to sleep, got up, and did the presentation. And you know what? It went great. It just flowed. It was more like a conversation than a presentation. We fostered a natural dialogue with the group, and we based the entire presentation on their needs in an effortless, conversational way. They loved it, and we had a great time being ourselves and sharing our knowledge.

Learning to listen to the voice of Personal Mastery is a lifelong development challenge. According to Virginia Satir, highly functional people tend to:

- See and hear what they see and hear, rather than what they are supposed to see and hear.

- Think what they think, rather than what they are supposed to think.
- Feel what they feel, rather than what they are supposed to feel.
- Want what they want, rather than what they are supposed to want.
- Imagine what they imagine, rather than what they are supposed to imagine.

Breaking Free of Self-Limiting Patterns

Joe Cavanaugh, in his wonderful retreats on self-esteem and personal mastery, tells a moving story about Peter, an elementary student who suffered burns on 90 percent of his body. Peter's burns were so severe that his mouth had to be propped open so it wouldn't seal shut in the healing process. His fingers were separated by splints so his hands wouldn't become webbed. His eyes were kept open so they wouldn't seal shut. Even after one year of rehabilitation and excruciating pain, Peter's spirit was intact. What was the first thing he did when he could walk? He helped console all the other patients by telling them that they would be all right, that they would get through it. His body may have been horribly burned, but his sense of self was whole.

Insights • Reflections • Commitments •

Eventually, Peter had to begin junior high at a new school. Imagine going to a new school at that age and being horribly disfigured. Imagine what the other kids would say and how they would react. On his first day in the cafeteria everyone avoided him. They looked at him with horror and then whispered to one another. Kids got up and moved from tables that were close to him. One student, Laura, had the courage to approach him and to introduce herself. As they talked and ate, she looked into Peter's eyes and sensed the person beneath the scarred surface. Reading her thoughts, Peter, in his deep, raspy, smoke-damaged voice, said, "Everyone is avoiding me because they don't know me yet. When they come to know me, they'll sit here with me. When they get to know the real me inside, they'll be my friends."

Peter was right. His character was so strong people eventually looked beyond the surface. People loved his spirit and wanted to be his friend.

Personal mastery means approaching one's life as a creative work, living life from a creative as opposed to reactive viewpoint.

—Peter Senge

When I consider Peter's situation, I'm not so sure that I would be able to come through his experiences with the same courage. But that's the beauty of Personal Mastery. Peter was challenged to awaken his extraordinary strength and to walk down his particular path. It was his path to master, not yours, not mine. Somehow his life had prepared him to walk that path with dignity. Although usually in a less dramatic fashion, each of us is challenged to master our own unique circumstances. Each of us is being called to lead by authentically connecting our own life experiences to the special circumstances we face. Our ability to rise to the challenge depends on our understanding of our own life experiences and how they have prepared us for our journey.

INTEGRATING ALL OF LIFE'S EXPERIENCES INTO A MEANINGFUL CONTEXT

Instead of cursing our past experiences, we need to value them as we begin the process of integrating our life experiences into a more meaningful context in the present. Personal Mastery is not a simplistic process of affirming our strengths while denying our weaknesses. It is about *growth toward wholeness*. It is about appreciating our gifts while unfolding underdeveloped or hidden sides of ourselves. It is about honestly facing and reconciling all our experiences. Personal Mastery involves appreciating the rich mixture of our life experiences and how they dynamically form our unique existence. Peter Senge, in *The Fifth Discipline,* wrote, "People with a high level of personal mastery are acutely aware of their ignorance, their incompetence, their growth areas, and they are deeply self-confident. Paradoxical? Only for those who do not see the journey is the reward."

GROWTH TOWARD WHOLENESS

One of the most effective ways to take this journey to a more integrated, complete understanding of ourselves is to explore deeply our personal belief system. Few psychological dynamics are as crucial as our beliefs. Beliefs literally create our reality; they are the lenses through which we interpret the world. Some of these "lenses" focus and open up new horizons; others dim our view and limit possibilities. Beliefs are transformational. Every belief we have transforms our life in either a life-enriching or life-limiting way.

INSIGHTS • REFLECTIONS
• COMMITMENTS •

One of the most dramatic examples of the transformational power of beliefs comes from heavyweight fighter George Foreman. In the 1970s, Foreman was renowned for being one of the toughest, nastiest human beings on the planet. He was not the person you see today. He was angry, antisocial, and not known for social graces or self-awareness. He was known as a tough, mean, uncommunicative person. Immediately following his surprising loss to Muhammad Ali in Zaire, he went to his dressing room, laid down on the training table and reportedly had an overwhelming spiritual experience. After that experience, he transformed his entire life. Everything changed: His personality, his relationships, his life purpose were all transformed into a more life-affirming direction. He peeled the onion of his personality and the delightful, humorous, self-effacing "George" came forward. The important thing to note here is not *if* George Foreman actually had a spiritual revelation. Many medical professionals said he suffered from severe heat exhaustion, and that's what caused his "experience." But that's not the issue. The key principle is that George Foreman *believed* he had a spiritual transformation and the belief changed his life. What we believe, we become.

When you empty yourself of the illusions of who and what you think you are, there is less to lose than you had feared.

—Carol Orsborn

AS YOU BELIEVE, SO SHALL YOU LEAD

Through my years of coaching people, I have observed consistently two distinct types of belief systems operating in people: *Conscious Beliefs* and *Shadow Beliefs*. Conscious Beliefs are the explicit, known beliefs we have. When asked about these beliefs about ourselves, about other people, or about life in general, we can articulate many of them. Even though it may take some effort to access and to clarify some of these beliefs, they are accessible to us on an everyday level. Examples of Conscious Beliefs someone might have are: "I believe in treating people with respect; I fear trying new things; I am creative and resilient; many people are untrustworthy; hard work brings results." Although we can access these beliefs on a conscious level, this does not mean we are always aware of them. However, we are usually aware of Conscious Beliefs and whether or not we are living according to those beliefs.

Take a few minutes and explore some of your Conscious Beliefs:

- What do you believe about yourself?
- What do you believe about other people?
- What do you believe about life?
- What do you believe about leadership?

Recently, we guided the chairman of the board of a fast-growing public company through the process of bringing his beliefs into conscious awareness. As a result, the 60-year-old chairman remarked, "Most people probably think I had this all figured out. What I discovered is that my beliefs were operating, but not consciously enough. After more than 30 years in leadership roles, I realize that unknowingly I had been inhibiting myself somewhat. Now I look forward to leading with conscious clarity and conviction." As we believe, so shall we lead.

Although we access Conscious Beliefs somewhat easily, Shadow Beliefs are subtler and often more challenging to uncover. Doing so, however, is crucial to high performance. Taken from the Jungian concept of "shadow," Shadow Beliefs are those beliefs which are manifestations of hidden, unexplored, or unresolved psychological dynamics. A Shadow Belief is cast when we don't want to deal with something. When a type of "secret" is held within us, a Shadow Belief is created.

INSIGHTS • REFLECTIONS • COMMITMENTS •

We all have Shadow Beliefs. If we don't think we do, then the shadow probably is operating at precisely that moment by obscuring a view of a portion of ourselves. Jeffrey Patnaude, in his work *Leading from the Maze,* writes, ". . . the leader must be awake and fully alert. Like a nighttime traveler attuned to every sound in the forest, the leader must be aware of all possibilities lurking in the shadows. For we can neither challenge nor transform what we cannot see."

On a personal level, some of my Shadow Beliefs have to do with exceptionally high standards for myself and others. From a young age, I evaluated myself by this external yardstick. As a result, I developed a series of Shadow Beliefs: "I'm never quite good enough; I have to work twice as hard to be valued; if something is not exceptional, it is not worthwhile." As you can see, these beliefs have some value. They have allowed me to be driven to achieve. On the other hand, some of these same beliefs cast a shadow on my behavior at times. However, as I've committed to constantly building my awareness of these shadows, I've been able to shed light on them, thereby minimizing their limiting influence.

Transforming Shadow Beliefs to Conscious Beliefs is crucial to Personal Mastery. This is not to say we don't struggle continually with them. We do. The difference is we consciously engage them versus unconsciously being driven by them. What happens to us if we don't deal with Shadow Beliefs? We pay a high price. Addictive behaviors, difficulty in relationships, imbalanced lifestyles, and health problems can be the costs associated with not dealing with them. Shadow Beliefs are not scary; not dealing with them is.

> *What you bring forth out of yourself from the inside will save you. What you do not bring forth out of yourself from the inside will destroy you.*
>
> —Gospel of Thomas

I remember coaching the president of a multibillion-dollar international firm who had a Shadow Belief that was limiting him. Steven was not referred to me because he had any "issues." He was wildly successful in his current role. In fact, it was his success that was starting to be a problem for him. He had this nagging anxiety—"Can I continue to top my past achievements?" Each time we would explore future plans, he would conjure up all sorts of disaster scenarios. As I got to know him better, I understood that he had internalized a hidden belief that no matter how hard he worked or what he achieved, it could all go away tomorrow. On one level this Shadow Belief served him well—it gave him the drive to achieve many goals. However, because he wasn't aware of it, his fear of failure was actually inhibiting him from risking new experiences and new learnings. Finally I asked Steven, "You don't get it, do you?" Surprised, he looked at me and said, "Get what?" I responded, "Steven, look at your life. Most everything you do succeeds. Your career, your family, your relationships. What evidence do you have that you are going to fail at your next endeavor?" It was a defining moment for Steven. He saw the shadow and brought it into the light. He moved from trusting his fear to trusting himself. He brought a Shadow Belief into the Conscious Belief arena. Before that moment he wasn't aware of its presence. It had been controlling him, and now he was beginning to take control of it. A few months later, describing his experience, he said, "This one insight has transformed my life. It has given me the peace of mind to trust myself and to lead from who I am. I now know that no matter what I attempt, I will make it a success."

SEVEN CLUES THAT BRING SHADOW BELIEFS TO LIGHT

How often have you heard the expression that "an overdeveloped strength can become a weakness"? Although there is some truth to this statement, it really does not capture the underlying dynamic. Why do some strengths turn into weaknesses? Usually because some Shadow Belief is operating. Leaders either shed light or cast a shadow on everything they do. The more conscious the self-awareness, the more light leaders bring. The more limited the self-understanding, the more shadows leaders cast. Let's say we have a Shadow Belief that "we only have value if we are doing and achieving." If we are unaware of this Shadow Belief, our drive and determination soon will turn into workaholism and lack of intimacy with profound negative implications for our health and relationships. Let's say we have self-confidence as a strength combined with a Shadow Belief that "we always have to be right." Without sufficient awareness, our self-confidence will turn into arrogance and abrasiveness. Here are some other examples of how shadows can potentially turn strengths into weaknesses:

INSIGHTS • REFLECTIONS • COMMITMENTS •

STRENGTH	POSSIBLE SHADOW BELIEF	WEAKNESS
Energy	"I can never give up"	Mania
Charm	"I must succeed— no matter what"	Manipulation
Conscientiousness	"I can always do better"	Compulsiveness
Focus	"I must know every detail to feel comfortable"	Narrowness/Rigidity
Courage	"I must always achieve more"	Foolhardiness

To leave our self-defeating behaviors behind we must use our conscious minds to undermine the destructive but unconscious beliefs that cause us to defeat ourselves.

—Milton Cudney and
Robert Hardy

Since our shadows are often hidden successfully from our own view, how can we bring them to light? Over the years we've developed seven clues to indicate if a shadow may be operating:

- *Shadow Clue One:* If other people often give us feedback inconsistent with how we see ourselves, a shadow is present.

- *Shadow Clue Two:* When we feel stuck or blocked with a real loss as to what to do next, a shadow is holding us back.

- *Shadow Clue Three:* As strengths become counterproductive, some hidden dynamics need to surface.

- *Shadow Clue Four:* When we are not open to new information, new learning, or other people's views, a shadow is limiting us.

- *Shadow Clue Five:* If we react to circumstances with emotional responses disproportionate to the situation, we are right over the target of a Shadow Belief.

- *Shadow Clue Six:* When we find ourselves forcefully reacting to the limitations of others in a critical, judgmental way, we are often projecting our unresolved shadow issues onto others.

- *Shadow Clue Seven:* If we often experience pain, trauma, or discomfort in our body, a shadow is attempting to rise to the surface to seek reconciliation. Listen to the wisdom of your body as you look to uncover Shadow Beliefs.

So what are the steps to master *conscious competence* regarding our beliefs?

- Work on bringing Conscious Beliefs to your awareness.

- Commit to the lifelong process of transforming Shadow Beliefs into Conscious Beliefs.

- Practice asking yourself about your Conscious and Shadow Beliefs.
  - What does this belief give me?
  - What does it open up?
  - What does this belief cost me?
  - What does it shut down?

- Practice reinforcing the beliefs that open you up to new possibilities.

- Practice deeply examining the consequences of beliefs that are damaging or limiting.

What happens to leaders who only acknowledge their strengths and attempt to conceal their weaknesses or mistakes? Many people perceive their weaknesses or mistakes and the leaders lose credibility. What happens to leaders who comprehend their strengths, weaknesses, and shadows and are not afraid to acknowledge them? People trust and follow these leaders.

INSIGHTS • REFLECTIONS • COMMITMENTS •

I remember working with an executive caught in this syndrome of infallible competence. He feared that revealing any of his limitations would result in others perceiving him as weak or inadequate. He also honestly believed others didn't perceive his underdeveloped side. After sharing with him a 360° assessment revealing how others saw his limitations even more clearly than he did, the coaching process began. Fortunately, after several months of coaching, a major business crisis surfaced. Here was the perfect opportunity to practice what he had learned. Clearly, he had made some mistakes leading up to the crisis. Rather than continuing the old pattern, he faced the troops, acknowledged his mistakes, and asked for their support. His co-workers were shocked, but they immediately rushed to his side and enthusiastically solved the crisis. Commenting on his experience, he told me, "I thought my power was in being *right*. Now I understand my power is in being *real*."

> *The ideal is in thyyself; the impediment, too, is in thyself.*
>
> —Thomas Carlyle

CHARACTER TRANSFORMS, PERSONA COPES

If *Leadership from the Inside Out* is *authentic self-expression* that creates value, how do we go about expressing ourselves more authentically? Since the word *authenticity* comes from the same Greek word as the word *author*, I'm sure no one would be surprised that authoring your own life does not have "ten easy steps." Authenticity requires a lifelong commitment to self-discovery and self-observation. However, in coaching leaders to unfold more authentic dimensions of self, we have found some helpful practices to bring out the essence of who we are. When a leader approaches the question, "How authentic am I?" it is often helpful to ask another question first: "Where is my leadership coming from?" We need to consider constantly the origin of our leadership in various circumstances. Do our actions originate from deep within ourselves, or are they coming from a more superficial, limited place? Is our leadership arising from our *Character*, the essence of who we are? Or, is it coming only from our *Persona*, the external personality we have created to cope with life circumstances?

Persona Primary—Character Secondary

This model represents a person who is principally guided by persona with a limited degree of character expressed. Persona is "thick and rigid," thereby "protecting" the individual. Opportunities for new learning are restricted from entering from the outside. New possibilities or potentialities are restricted from being expressed from within. This diagram illustrates leading and living from a superficial, non-authentic level.

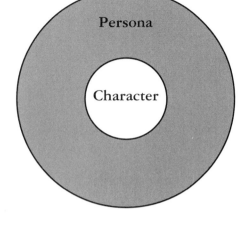

Character Primary—Persona Secondary

This model represents a person who is principally guided by character. Persona is thin, flexible, and permeable. Opportunities for learning more readily flow in from the outside and possibilities and potentialities are expressed from the inside. This diagram illustrates leading and living from a deeper, more authentic level.

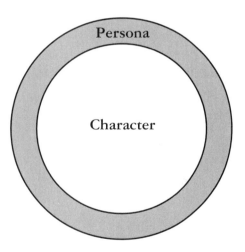

Character is the essence, the being of the leader, which is deeper and broader than any action or achievement. It is the essential nature of the person. In his essay on character, Ralph Waldo Emerson wrote, "This is what we call character—a reserved force which acts directly as presence, and without means."

The purpose of character is to transform and to open up possibilities and potentialities. Qualities of character include authenticity, purpose, openness, trust, congruence, compassion, and creating value. When we are In-Character, we transform circumstances and open up possibilities and potentialities.

Persona is the personality or "mask" we wear to cope with our life experiences. Persona is built to "protect us" from external stressors, as well as internal fears, limitations, and inadequacies. Our external shell can be either rigid and thick, preventing new possibilities to enter or to arise, or it can be permeable, thin and flexible, allowing learning and expression of potentialities.

Once leaders commit to doing the deeply personal work of cutting through the layers of ego, they begin to clarify how to make an authentic contribution in all their spheres of influence.

—Tom Gegax

The purpose of the persona is to "protect us" and help us cope. Qualities of the persona include image, safety, security, comfort, control, fear, and winning at all costs. When we are In-Persona we seek to cope with circumstances. Even though many influences and circumstances in our life are far beyond our control, we do control our choices. We are free to be whatever we want. We can be ourselves or not. We can be true to ourselves or not. We can wear one mask now and another one later, and never, if we choose, appear in our true face. With these choices also come great costs. We may actually identify with the "mask" as our true self. Then later, we wonder at crucial moments why we lack effectiveness; or why truth evades us; or why life does not make sense; or why life lacks fulfillment or purpose. Our choice is free, but the consequences of not following the path to authenticity are great.

QUALITIES GUIDING CHARACTER AND PERSONA

As leaders it is essential to learn how to build our awareness of when we are being guided by character and when we are being guided by persona. The following information reveals some of the qualities that guide character and persona:

CHARACTER:	PERSONA:
Leading from the Inside Out	*Leading on the Outside*
Transforms: Opens up possibilities and potentialities	Protects/Copes: Limits possibilities and potentialities
Guided By: Authenticity	Guided By: Image

Purpose	Safety/Security
Openness	Control
Trust	Fear
Compassion	Self-Interest
Courage	Avoidance
Inclusion	Exclusion
Creating Value and Contribution	Winning at All Costs
Balance/Centeredness	Distraction
Fluidity/Adaptability	Resistance to Change
Peaceful Presence	Uneasy Presence
Being Supporting Doing	Doing Supporting More Doing

Let's explore three examples:

1. Image vs. Authenticity: If we are guided principally by image, we are In-Persona. We are in the image persona when we misrepresent the reality of our experience, or the truth of our being; when we present ourselves as more than we are; or when we fake values or beliefs to win acceptance. Recently, I was coaching the CEO of a firm and one of his key executives. Although the CEO needed to work on a few crucial growth areas, authenticity was not one of them. The key executive in his organization, however unknowingly, was caught up in her image. At a critical point in one of their interactions as the key executive was overanalyzing all the political implications of an important decision, the CEO calmly and compassionately asked, "Michelle, do you want to look good, or do you want to make a difference?" Michelle fell silent. Of course she wanted to make a differ-

INSIGHTS • REFLECTIONS • COMMITMENTS •

ence. She needed someone to shock her out of investing herself totally in persona and into shifting her awareness to leading from character. In *The Corporate Mystic*, Gay Hendricks and Kate Ludeman reinforce this practice: "It is as important to challenge people about their personas as it is to love and cherish their true essence. In the business world it is dangerous to ignore people's personas. Genuinely caring for people means seeing them as they are, not blithely over-looking fatal flaws."

Corporate Mystics develop a kind of double vision, at once able to see the mask and the essential person inside. . . . They know that we all have personas that are wrapped around our true essence, but they also know that we are not our personas.

—Gay Hendricks and
Kate Ludeman

2. Safety, Security, and Comfort vs. Purpose: If our actions are principally guided by safety, security, and comfort, we are In-Persona. This is a big one for most of us. It is also subtle. We are usually unaware of how staying safe is actually limiting us from new experiences and possibilities. How often have most of us thought, "When I build up enough assets, then I'll go do what I *really* want to do?" This is the voice of persona. In the executive ranks this is a major issue. As senior executives seek to become more comfortable financially and otherwise, do they continue to risk innovative, meaningful, out-of-the-box initiatives? Often they do not.

I was working with a senior marketing executive who was caught in this persona pattern. The first day I met Jack he told me he had lost his passion for his work and was preparing to leave his organization to seek a new career. After spending some time together, he shared his career-life vision: to accumulate assets in order to replace his current income and in five years start his own business. On the surface it sounded all right. As we went deeper, however, it became apparent that he had sacrificed his purpose on the altar of security and comfort. Driven by his need to accumulate money in an attempt to build his inner sense of security, he gradually had lost touch with what really gave him meaning: making a difference through helping others achieve their potential. Once Jack got reconnected to his purpose, he returned to his work with renewed passion and perspective.

When we are caught up In-Persona, we seek solutions outside of ourselves like changing a job, changing a career, accumulating enough money to feel secure, and so forth. Too often we seek solutions in "Whats" instead of "Hows." Jack needed to re-learn *how* to show up in his life in a renewed way. He learned how to be On-Purpose and In-Character.

3. Control vs. Openness: If our life energies are absorbed in control, we are In-Persona. This is particularly challenging if we are moving from managerial to leadership roles in an organization. Managers control by virtue of their *doing.* Leaders lead by virtue of their *being.* When we are (as is often the case) rapidly alternating between management and leadership, the relationship between control and openness is a constant dynamic.

INSIGHTS • REFLECTIONS • COMMITMENTS •

Tracy, a senior-level executive for an international service firm, was clearly identified with her "control" persona. She viewed herself as an exceptionally competent person, and by all external measures she was. Based on a series of outstanding achievements in sales and marketing, she had been on the fast track in her company. She was known for always exceeding the need. If the organization wanted something done exceptionally well, Tracy was the one they recruited for the job. Some would say she had mastered her profession—maybe even mastered some aspects of her external environment. But her external success was not based on internal mastery. Her obsessive need to control everything around her had created strain in all her relationships. Her marriage wasn't surviving her need to control. Her children were growing distant. Her friendships were suffering. The more Tracy's life started to spin out of control, the more she tried to assert control.

Without understanding why, she gradually drove away nearly everyone around her. For many years, her external competence had been sufficient to face her life and career demands. However, her new life and leadership demands involved competence of a different order. Before Tracy could move to this next stage of leadership and life effectiveness, she needed to access a platform of internal competence and character.

The leader for today and the future will be focused on how to be—how to develop quality, character, mind-set, values, principles, and courage.

—Frances Hesselbein

It took a few months of coaching, but she came to the realization that her excessive need to control was based on a Shadow Belief. She had come to believe that just being herself and trusting that things would work out was not an option for her. At a crucial point in our coaching she said, "If I stopped controlling everything, my life would fall apart!" The instant she said it, the paradox hit her with full force. Her life *was* falling apart because she was so controlling. Yet, she felt that control was her only savior. Over time, she gained the Personal Mastery to begin trusting and to be more open to change. As her self-trust and openness grew, her ability to trust and to appreciate others grew as well. She had begun her path to leading In-Character and living "from the inside out."

It's important to note that the two columns of qualities listed in the Character-Persona chart on pages 44–45 do not necessarily oppose one another. For instance, fear might be the quality of persona keeping us from authenticity; or control may be inhibiting us from openness in our character; or safety may be preventing us from developing compassion. These are only three examples. In life, any number or combination of persona qualities could be impacting one or any combination of character qualities. Take some time to review the rest of the qualities that guide character and persona on pages 44–45. Spend some time considering the qualities of persona:

- When are you guided by these qualities?
- What is going on in those times?
- How do you feel?
- What fears, limitations, or inadequacies do you avoid when you are In-Persona?
- How can you challenge yourself to move out of persona and into character more often?

Now, reflect on the qualities of character:

- When are you guided by these qualities?
- What is going on in those times?
- How do you feel?
- What fears do you have to face to get In-Character?
- How can you continue to be In-Character in more situations in the future?

INSIGHTS • REFLECTIONS • COMMITMENTS •

As we have seen, character transforms while persona copes. When we are In-Persona we tend to see the problems of life as existing outside of ourselves. We say to ourselves, "If I could only change this person or that situation, then everything would be fine." But life's problems are rarely resolved by only changing the external situation. Lasting solutions involve dealing with our internal situation in order to transform the external circumstance. To illustrate this principle, imagine Nelson Mandela a few years ago saying, "I think I need to leave South Africa. The situation here is just too big a problem. These people just don't get it. I need to go to a more comfortable, accommodating country." It sounds humorous even to imagine a scenario from a person of such character. When character and purpose are weak, then our initial coping response is usually to leave or escape our situation. When purpose is strong, leaders transform many of the circumstances they encounter. Obviously we need to leave some situations for purposes of self-preservation. However, if our first response is consistently to exit challenging circumstances, then we probably need to work on unfolding character.

I have often thought that the best way to define a man's character would be to seek out the particular mental or moral attitude in which, when it came upon him, he felt himself deeply and intensively active and alive. At such moments, there is a voice inside which speaks and says, "This is the real me."

—William James

It's important to note that Personal Mastery is not about eliminating persona. It is about increasing character to such a degree that character is primary and persona is secondary. Persona exists for a reason—to protect and to cope—so we really don't want to eliminate it completely. It serves a purpose. But we do want to unfold character so that this essence of life flows through us as our principal guiding force. To have character supporting persona—the inner supporting the outer—is the goal of Personal Mastery.

Leading from character is not easy. The CEO of a rapidly growing firm shared this comment with me: "I hate to admit it, but most organizations reward persona. We talk about character, but we reward persona. We extol the values of trust, inclusion, and adding value, but we consistently reward control and image. Most of us are unwilling to do the hard work and to take the personal risk to lead from character."

Unfortunately, executive coaching programs often reinforce refining persona rather than unfolding character. Executives are coached *how to act* instead of *how to be*. It's a charm-school process that produces only superficial, short-term results. Executives are "coached" to polish up the exterior, but rarely does any real substantial growth take place. Under sufficient stress all the old patterns return.

To be effective, executive coaching needs to cut through persona—make it more permeable—so character can surface. Penetrating persona to allow character to come forth requires sophisticated coaching that considers the whole person.

Understanding Our Owner's Manual

Many of us know more about our favorite vacation spot, sports team, or running shoes than we do about ourselves. In order to break out of old patterns and grow as a whole person, we need to answer the "Who am I?" question. We may get snickers from our own inner "peanut gallery." Or we may return with a quick answer that superficially reflects the roles we play versus who we really are.

The other day I sat down with a CEO for an initial coaching session. With a bit of nervous bravado the executive proclaimed, "Kevin, you know, I know myself pretty well." I've been in situations like this so many times that I felt like a subtitle should appear underneath him that would read, "He doesn't know himself very well." On the other hand, when I meet with someone who shares, "You know, I understand some aspects of myself, but others are still a mystery to me," then the subtext would say, "This person knows himself pretty well." I think the reason most people think they know themselves well is that their experience of their inner world is restricted to very narrow boundaries. Few people would admit that they know everything *outside* of themselves. We all understand how unfathomable external knowledge and information is. We see the external world as huge. Our inner life, however, is

INSIGHTS • REFLECTIONS
• COMMITMENTS •

defined too often in a very restricted way. When we get on the path to Personal Mastery, we begin to glimpse how deep, broad, and unbounded our inner life really is. When people casually say, "I know myself," all too often they are really saying, "I know my limited state of self-knowledge." There are no limits within us. There is no end to Personal Mastery. It is bigger, deeper and grander than the external world we think is so vast. Begin your journey by considering life's big questions: "Who are you? Where are you headed? Why are you going there?" That darn soldier just crossed our path again, didn't he?

Just trust yourself, then you will know how to live.

—Goethe

Personal Mastery is about comprehending the vehicle, our character, that brings us to our destination. There's just one problem: We've temporarily lost the "owner's manual." It's like buying a high performance sports car without learning how to drive it. Sure we know how to drive—we just don't understand how to drive *that* vehicle. How are we ever going to arrive safely at our desired destination when we don't understand that taking a curve at sixty-five miles an hour on a wet road at midnight with a certain suspension system is an invitation for disaster? That's exactly how we live our lives—barreling down the freeway of life without any real mastery of our owner's manual. So how can we start to understand our owner's manual? How can we begin to uncover our identity and maneuver this "vehicle"? The following reflection will help you get on the path. But remember, no one else can give you this insight. You must give it to yourself. This is the beginning of the process.

REFLECTION

PERSONAL MASTERY

Clarifying Our Strengths and Growth Areas

Take your time. Be thoughtful. The questions are designed to be thought-provoking, so don't rush through them. Read all of the questions first, and begin the exercise by answering the ones that come easiest. Use a notepad to sketch out longer responses.

1. Imagine yourself observing a dear friend talking about you with heartfelt love and admiration. What would your friend be saying?

2. When you are energized and inspired, what particular personality traits or strengths are being expressed by you?

3. What are some of your Conscious Beliefs about yourself?

4. What are some of your Shadow Beliefs about yourself?

5. When you are In-Character, what qualities come forth? Do certain situations inhibit or express your character more?

6. When you are In-Persona, what qualities come forth? What beliefs or fears are generating these qualities?

7. When in your life have you felt most completely yourself—not meeting others' expectations, but just being fulfilled in expressing who you are?

8. What steps can you take in your life to create more times like this?

9. You are a never-to-be repeated leader. What combination of life experiences, life challenges and innate character traits have uniquely prepared you?

10. If you had to write a eulogy for your own funeral, what would it say?

TIME OUT. It's time for commitment. Rather than treating this book as another interesting, intellectual journey, it's time to genuinely commit yourself to growth. Commitment is the bridge that connects inner insight to outer achievement. As David Prosser, Chairman of RTW, shared with me, "Commitment is what makes the impossible possible." Without explicit commitments, you may just breeze through this book, touching on a few great insights and then *nothing happens to transform your life*. Commitment is the springboard from which we launch all significant transformation; it propels intention into effective action.

LEADERSHIP GROWTH
COMMITMENTS

PERSONAL MASTERY

Reflect on the learnings that have surfaced as you read this chapter. Identify three leadership growth commitments to enhance your self-knowledge and personal mastery. Then identify the potential obstacles, resources needed, and signs or measures of success. (See sample which follows.)

1. Key Learnings:
A. _____
B. _____
C. _____

2. Leadership Growth Commitments:
A. _____
B. _____
C. _____

3. Resources Needed:
A. _____
B. _____
C. _____

4. Potential Obstacles:
A. _____
B. _____
C. _____

5. Timeline and Measures of Success:
A. _____
B. _____
C. _____

LEADERSHIP GROWTH COMMITMENTS

PERSONAL MASTERY SAMPLE

1. Key Learnings: *My image and control personas are more prevalent than I thought; need to build awareness of my self-limiting belief regarding "never achieving/doing enough."*

2. Leadership Growth Commitments:

A. *Move from control persona to trust to let others participate more.*

B. *Let go of some of my image needs.*

C. *Explore my need to do so much.*

3. Resources Needed:

A. *Consider 360° feedback.*

B. *Explore coaching resources.*

C. *Get colleague, spouse participation.*

4. Potential Obstacles:

A. *Fear of change.*

B. *Fear of failure if I change things too much.*

C. *Will colleagues/organization accept changes?*

5. Timeline and Measures of Success:

A. *In 3 months, having people acknowledge that I am less controlling.*

B. *In 6 months, having several people notice that I am dropping my image and being more authentic.*

C. *In 1 month, getting home before 6:30 p.m., 4 nights a week.*

SEVEN POINTS OF AWARENESS FOR LEADING THROUGH AUTHENTIC SELF-EXPRESSION

Keep in mind the following principles as you begin to master your ability to lead through authentic self-expression.

*1. **Take Total Responsibility:*** Commit yourself to the path of Personal Mastery. Only you can commit to it, and only you can walk your own path to it. No one else can motivate you. No one else can do it for you. A mentor cannot do it for you. Your organization or clients cannot do it for you. As Hermann Hesse wrote in *Demian*, "Each man had only one genuine vocation—to find the way to himself. . . . His task was to discover his own destiny—not an arbitrary one—and live it out wholly and resolutely within himself. Everything else was only a would-be existence, an attempt at evasion, a flight back to the ideals of the masses, conformity, and fear of one's own inwardness." Personal Mastery is the one life experience you must give yourself. No one else is "in the loop." In fact, no one else can be in the loop for it to be genuine. Walt Whitman wrote, "Not I— not anyone else—can travel that road for you; you must learn to travel it for yourself."

At first, this may be difficult. Learning to assume total responsibility for your life is no small task. Keep reminding yourself that you are it. No one else is responsible for your happiness, fulfillment, satisfaction, competence, health, or life situation but you. No matter what life or leadership challenges you face, you are not a victim of your

INSIGHTS • REFLECTIONS • COMMITMENTS •

circumstances; you are responsible. As you advance, you will find that you feel happy for no particular reason—no external event has validated you—you just are feeling good about being *you*. As you increasingly assume responsibility for yourself, you are prepared to assume responsibility for leading others. All leadership begins with self-leadership and self-responsibility.

To contact the deeper truth of who we are, we must engage in some activity or practice that questions what we assume to be true about ourselves.

—A. H. Almaas

2. *Bring Beliefs to Conscious Awareness:* Commit to the process of clarifying your Conscious Beliefs and unfolding your Shadow Beliefs. Practice by reflecting on how some of these beliefs open you up and how others close you down. Practice reinforcing the ones that open up possibilities and examining the consequences of the ones that limit you. Constantly remind yourself of the *Leadership from the Inside Out* mantra: "As you believe, so shall you lead."

3. *Develop Awareness of Character and Persona:* Develop an awareness of when you are being guided by the qualities of character and when you are being guided by the qualities of persona. Instead of investing in persona, commit your energies to unfolding character. Doing so requires that you courageously examine the beliefs, fears, and limitations generating the qualities of persona. Facing these limiting filters will free up energy to experience new learning from the outside, as well as to express new potentiality from within. Transform your approach to leading by making character primary and persona secondary.

4. *Practice Personal Mastery with Others:* Practicing Personal Mastery is not always an easy task. It requires risk. It requires placing ourselves in situations where we may not be accepted or validated by others for who we are or what we believe. If we do not take this risk, we will always be living our lives for others and delivering to them what they are looking for. As a result, we compromise our integrity. If you find yourself constantly reading the environment to deliver the desired response, then you may need lots of practice. As you practice Personal Mastery with others, keep these thoughts in mind:

- Listen to your authentic inner voice for what *you* really think and feel versus what others want you to think and feel.
- Seek to avoid "creating" others in your own image.
- Seek to avoid "being created" by others in their image.
- Enjoy the validation and support from others when it comes to you, but do not expect it or be disappointed if it does not happen. It is your job to validate your authentic self.
- Avoid judging others or trying to change them—it is a waste of time.
- Be there for people when they need you. Be there—not for the purpose of giving advice or being appreciated for your support—but just to be there for them.
- Practice sharing your genuine thoughts and feelings, your joys, your successes, your concerns, and your fears with people. You will be amazed how your life will be enriched.

INSIGHTS • REFLECTIONS
• COMMITMENTS •

5. *Listen to Feedback:* Even though Personal Mastery is self-validating, sometimes other people hold keys to our self-knowledge.

How often have we resisted the input of others only to realize later that their comments were revealing? Is it possible their insights were greater than we were prepared to assimilate? Rather than spending our energy defending a rigid state of self, we can think of Personal Mastery as a continually unfolding process. Life experiences are there to develop us. People are there to teach us. Consider all input from others as potentially instructive. Sometimes those around us light our path to Personal Mastery.

6. Consider Finding a Coach: There is nothing "wrong" with getting support. Having a coach as your partner during your growth process might be the most "right" thing you ever do. You might be pleasantly surprised to know how much an objective, experienced coach can accelerate your personal and leadership progress. Coaching can free up self-knowledge and facilitate some helpful directions for growth.

> *No man is free who is not a master of himself.*
>
> —Epictetus

Be sure to take some time. Initially, have personal sessions with a few people. Share your story and then gauge your chemistry and values connections with each potential coach. Quality professional support can offer a significant growth experience. It is a time to be yourself and get the objective support you need.

7. Be Flexible: Sometimes the strengths that helped you lead in your present state of development may hamper your future chances of success.

You may recall the news photos of Karl Wallenda's final high-wire performance as he attempted to cross two tall buildings. As he made his way on the wire, using his famous balancing pole, an intense wind came up. Everyone watching immediately understood Wallenda's dilemma. As the wind blew him off the wire, he clutched onto his balancing pole. All he needed to do was to let go of the pole and grab the wire. But, because the pole had saved his balance so many times before, he held onto it even as he fell to the ground. He held onto what he knew best even when it no longer served him. Understand and appreciate your strengths, but also be flexible and adaptable. Many strong winds may be coming your way.

PERSONAL MASTERY SUMMARY

• *Take Total Responsibility:* No one else can validate your value. It is for you to give yourself. Leaders can effectively validate and support others only if they have validated themselves first.

• *Practice Personal Mastery with Others:* Risk sharing your genuine thoughts and feelings with others. Avoid "creating others" in your image or being "created by others" in their image. Lead with your own original voice.

• *Bring Beliefs to Conscious Awareness:* Clarify Conscious Beliefs and uncover Shadow Beliefs. Practice reinforcing the ones that open up possibilities and setting aside the ones that limit you. As you believe, so shall you lead.

• *Develop Awareness of Character and Persona:* Commit to being guided by the qualities of character. Character transforms, persona copes. Transform how you lead and how you live by making character primary and persona secondary.

• *Listen to Feedback:* Sometimes other people hold keys to unlocking self-knowledge. Rather than spending energy resisting feedback, look for the seeds of learning contained in people's perceptions. Leaders grow proportionally to their openness to input.

• *Consider Finding a Coaching Process:* Seek objective coaching support to accelerate your growth as a leader. Willingly partner with an expert in personal growth much as you partner with experts regarding business issues.

• *Be Flexible:* Overdeveloped strengths may work against you as things change. Be prepared to take a fresh approach. Be open to drawing out new personal potentialities to prepare for future leadership challenges.

PATHWAY TWO: PURPOSE MASTERY

Leading by Expressing Our Gifts to Create Value

Purpose Mastery is the ongoing discovery of how we express our gifts to add life-enriching value to the world.

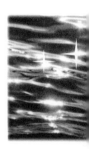

Why is one of the most powerful words in our language. "Why?" is the question that calls us to meaning; it forces us to look beneath the surface into the deeper essence of things. "Why?" is the question that directs us onto the path of purpose.

THE POWER OF WHY

Several months ago, our firm was engaged to help select a senior executive for an international company. A slate of top internal candidates needed to be interviewed and assessed to ensure the optimal decision for all parties. One of the top candidates was an exceptional woman. She had outstanding credentials and a solid track record. As I was interviewing her, it became obvious to me that she was exceedingly driven by achievement. Each of her descriptions focused on moving quickly from one achievement to another; she barely could catch her breath as she outlined them. As I listened, I sensed that something was missing. She easily elaborated her accomplishments, but a deeper sense of fulfillment, satisfaction, and passion was absent.

At a crucial moment, when she had nearly finished sharing her career highlights, I asked her what she wanted to achieve next. Without even pausing to reflect for an instant, her achievement drive focused on the senior executive position at hand. I then asked her the really tough question, "Why?" She was speechless—completely stunned. As she struggled to give me a rational response, she knew she did not have an answer. Achievement had become her only reason for being. Her purpose, the meaning behind her achievements, was temporarily lost.

Two weeks passed before I met with her again. At this next meeting, she seemed somewhat disturbed. Finally, she said, "I've been really struggling with the 'Why?' question you asked me. I still don't have an answer. But I am now committed to finding out." The Power of Why led her to the path of Mastery of Purpose.

Work is the very fire where we are baked to perfection, and like the master of the fire itself, we add the essential ingredient and fulfillment when we walk into the flames ourselves.

—David Whyte

How are you doing with the "Why" questions in your life? Why are you motivated to achieve? Does your answer reflect your values as an entire person or does it only represent a small portion of who you are? Spend some time with the "Why" questions: Why do you lead the way you do? Why do you live the lifestyle you do? Why do you have the relationships you do? Spending time with these questions can be revealing. You may discover a deeper level of meaning for you, and become aware of what is missing.

THE POWER OF HOW

Although the "Why" question can get you on the path to meaning, answering the "How" question can reveal purpose. Too often, our reason for being is seen as a "What." How often have we heard or said, "*What* are you going to be when you grow up?" Rarely, if ever, do we challenge ourselves or others to consider, "*How* are you going to be when you grow up?" *What* is the external manifestation of purpose. *How* is the internal process of purpose.

If leadership is authentic self-expression that creates value, then purpose is how we express ourselves to add value. As my colleague, David Brings, shared with me, "At the moment we come to know and accept all that has happened in our lives, the possibilities open up—we come to know our purpose in the simple and authentic mindfulness of how we have been, how we now 'show up' in the world, and how we want to become."

BEYOND MAKING A DIFFERENCE

I was working with an executive recently who told me he had his purpose all worked out. When I asked him to describe his purpose, he confidently said, "To make a difference." He was a bit disappointed when I said, "Well, that's a start, but a drug dealer makes a difference, too—it just happens to be a life-damaging one." Struggling he said, "You know what I meant." I responded, "No, I don't know what you meant. That's the point; your meaning is absent from your purpose. The real question is, 'How do you express your gifts to make a difference in all parts of your life?'"

INSIGHTS • REFLECTIONS • COMMITMENTS •

There once was a leader of a major monastery in China who was known for his purposeful teaching. However, instead of lecturing people on his teachings and getting lost in theory and concept, he would demonstrate his purposefulness by sweeping the steps of the monastery with all his being. People would come to the entry inquiring about the leader of the monastery and the "sweeper" would say, "The teacher is teaching now." Since most of the aspirants were focused on looking for something external, "the teacher," they rarely recognized that the entire teaching and meaning were present in *how* the sweeper approached his work-life.

Purpose is present in *how we show up* in whatever activity we engage. As a leader, how are you showing up? Are you lecturing others about how things should be, or are you purposefully leading by example? Is only part of your being in your work, or is all your being present in how you lead?

UNFOLDING THE DEFINING THREAD OF PURPOSE

You may think that I have "this purpose thing" all figured out. Actually, the only thing I know for sure is that it's an endless journey. A few years ago, I was convinced about the value of purpose, yet my own purpose was not crystal-clear to me. I began to take my own advice. Over and over I asked myself two crucial questions, "Why do I pursue the work-life I do?" and "How do I show up during the most fulfilling, energetic times in my life?" Again and again, I explored these questions.

Purpose is the idée fixe, *the recurring theme, the touchstone of self that flows beneath the surface, like an underground spring, nourishing the continuous and future expressions of who we are.*

—David Brings

Over time, glimpses of this elusive "thing" called purpose emerged. Sometimes in a quiet moment an insight would come. Other times, while I was working, I would feel its presence. Occasionally a glimpse would appear in a personal relationship. As the months passed, an awareness started to unfold. One day I was running along one of my favorite wooded trails beside a creek. I wasn't trying to sort things out, but my "defining thread" was rolling out like a ball of yarn thrown across the floor. This "thread" seemed to connect all the significant experiences of my life: Whether I was seeking my education in psychology, teaching people how to meditate, being a career consultant, being an executive coach, it was all about one thing: *Being a catalyst for personal awakening.* The insight was so clear it actually stopped me in my tracks. Absorbed in the power of this realization, I assimilated this "connecting thread." It was a defining moment. My purpose had always been operating, but the power of the moment was bringing it to conscious awareness. From that point forward, my life had more *conscious context.* Decisions no longer seemed ambiguous or reactive. I started to understand why I was doing the things I was doing and how I was expressing my gifts to make a contribution. My reason for being was starting to come into focus.

One of the most amazing things about purpose is that it is operating every-where. Nothing happens without purpose. A seed would never sprout. The planets in the heavens would not move in perfect symmetry. The laws of nature would cease to function. The artist would not paint. The musician would not play music. The leader would not lead. Purpose gives meaning and direction to all of life. Without purpose, we cease to be. As Goethe put it, "A life without purpose is an early death." The lack of meaning or purpose could be the critical missing element in our world today. When we look at all the external challenges we face—crime, violence, drugs, unemployment, the breakdown of the family—they all are symptomatic of one thing: disconnection from our inner meaning and purpose.

Consider for a moment that lack of purpose is the principal threat we face today. Why does one child in the inner city transcend his or her circumstances and create a productive, fulfilling life while another child gets caught up in a downward spiral of drugs and crime? Purpose may be the only adequate protection we have to ensure that we rise above our circumstances. Why does one unemployed person view her situation as an opportunity to connect with what she always wanted to do while another person sees his situation as a hopeless disaster? Why does one leader see possibilities while another sees only problems?

INSIGHTS • REFLECTIONS • COMMITMENTS •

THE CONTEXT THAT FRAMES LEADERSHIP

Purpose is the context that frames all of our life experiences into a meaningful whole. If we have it, all the challenging experiences of life serve to forge our identity and character. Although life may be challenging, every experience is our teacher, and every challenge an opportunity to live more purposefully. If we lack purpose, our immediate circumstances dominate our awareness and overshadow our reason for being. As a result, our life tends to lose connection with its true nature. Teilhard de Chardin wrote, "We are not human beings having a spiritual experience. We are spiritual beings having a human experience." Purpose is spirit seeking expression; awareness of it allows us to clearly see our lives from the inside out.

> *Purpose is the most essential core of leadership. Without purpose there is no mission, vision, or reason for being.*
>
> —Tom Votel

You may be thinking that all this seems a bit abstract and esoteric. However, purpose may be the most practical, useful connection to an effective life. It is often the most crucial variable in personal and leadership effectiveness. Because purpose is transformational, it converts average-performing organizations, families, or relationships into highly effective ones. It transforms employees, spouses, or friends into co-partners. With purpose, managers become leaders.

PURPOSE IS A DISCOVERY, NOT A GOAL

In our leadership development practice, we often work with executives who excel in the technical, managerial, and functional aspects of their work but need to develop further their ability to connect with people. They are great managers but need to unfold the personal power and inspiration to lead effectively. What's missing? Usually these people have lost their connection to their principles, beliefs, and passionate purposes. Once they discover their purposeful potential, they are transformed from managers to leaders. It's important to note that no personality change is necessary. What is required is a commitment to discover purpose and to grow to a new level of personal potential and expression. The same principles for leading apply to us in all areas of our life—family, community, business, ourselves—it's all about living our life congruent with our principles, beliefs, and character. As author and consultant Richard Leider would say, it's about living "on-purpose."

After twenty-seven years with a major insurance company, Ray was terminated. Even though he never really loved his work, it was still a major blow to his identity and sense of self. His day of termination seemed like a bad dream.

Reflecting on that day he said, "I felt like a candle which had been snuffed out." The world looked pretty dark, and he felt powerless. In spite of our early attempts to provide support, he just wasn't open to it. For a few weeks he disengaged from the world and absorbed himself in a victimized view of his situation. Fortunately one day his granddaughter approached him with the penetrating innocence that only a child can exhibit and said, "Grandpa, are you okay?" It was just the mirror he needed, and he immediately started to sob deeply. For the first time, he could admit his pain and acknowledge that he needed some help.

At his first few coaching sessions, it became obvious to me that Ray was a passionate, principle-driven leader. Unfortunately, his passion had not been to run an insurance operation. One day I said to him, "Ray, what would you *really love to do*?" He responded, "All my life people have told me I should be a minister. I would love to dedicate my life to helping people spiritually." Once he renewed his sense of purpose, everything changed. His unemployment was no longer a hopeless situation. In fact, it became the means for connecting him to his lifelong dream. He converted his hopeless view of the world into a meaningful, exciting possibility. His sense of self not only returned, but was renewed. Within four months, he became the Executive Director of a major church association. His new role offered him the opportunity to integrate his values, purpose, and management expertise. Through Mastery of Purpose he transformed his entire life.

INSIGHTS • REFLECTIONS • COMMITMENTS •

Purpose is not a goal to be set. It is not something you create. It is not some "great idea" you come up with. It is something you discover. Purpose is there all the time, and it's calling for you. It's your duty, it's your role in life, it's what you have been prepared to express. As Joe Jaworski writes in *Synchronicity—The Inner Path of Leadership*, "It is the call to service, giving our life over to something larger than ourselves, the call to become what we were meant to become—the call to achieve our *vital design*." If we ignore this calling, no amount of external success can make us feel complete.

Purpose is the still point— the peaceful center around which all dynamic leadership revolves.

—Rob Hawthorne

The implications of discovering purpose go far beyond our profession or career. They impact all of our life. A client of ours discovered that her life's purpose was "to use her influencing and counseling gift to be of service to people." While this purpose potentially could influence all sorts of career outcomes in teaching, consulting, professional associations, non-profit groups or business in general, it also would impact her personal, spiritual, and community life. Purpose is the broad context that integrates all of our life experiences. It is the *defining thread* that runs through and connects life's divergent experiences.

Jack Hawley writes in *Reawakening the Spirit in Work*, "Our life direction is about moving into the vacant upstairs flat." Purpose is that home within, that place where our values and spirit reside. It's there all the time, waiting for our arrival. We may have been too busy "living our life downstairs" to even notice.

"MOVING UPSTAIRS" TO OUR PURPOSE

A few years ago, I worked with a client who recently realized that she had been "living downstairs." She entered my office in a down mood and after very little chitchat blurted out, "Cake mixes don't give any meaning to my life!" Caught off guard, I started laughing. She wasn't amused and said, "I'm serious; I used to love my job, but it just doesn't seem important to me anymore." After I worked with her for a while, she began to explore the contents of her "upstairs flat." Her discovery centered around "using her creative and conceptual gifts to add value to people's lives." She had been "living downstairs" for so long that she actually thought that cake mixes were supposed to give meaning to her life! Her purpose became overshadowed by her day-to-day focus. When she finally uncovered her purpose, her attitude about her job changed, her creativity returned, and her performance soared. Her life wasn't about cake mixes; it was about being a creative force to enhance people's lives. This realization permeated her entire life situation, and everyone in her life sensed her renewal.

DIVING BENEATH THE SURFACE TO OUR PURPOSE

Unfortunately, most people tend to limit purpose by viewing it as something external. To really understand the value of purpose we need to dive beneath the surface.

INSIGHTS • REFLECTIONS • COMMITMENTS •

I worked once with the president of a large company who was struggling with purpose and meaning in his life. Even though he had strong family values and other interests, he was having a difficult time comprehending his life's purpose as something bigger than his career. All his life he had aspired to achieve his current career goal. Along the way he had made many difficult personal sacrifices to achieve it. Now that he had achieved his "purpose" he was feeling, "Is this it?"

Although my client had a vague sense that there must be more than his achieved goal, he couldn't articulate what it was. At one of our sessions I asked him, "What happens when a company defines itself by its products and results instead of its underlying competencies and values?" He immediately responded, "Well, they eventually perish because, as the marketplace changes, their products become obsolete." I then said,

"What happens to the company that defines itself by its core values and capabilities?" He again quickly responded, "They thrive because they continually adapt themselves to the changing market." Then I said, "So, which type of 'company' are you?" He immediately became aware of how his external definition was limiting him. He realized that his purpose was not about simply achieving the next career goal. His passion was deeper than that. It was about helping people to grow. His entire personal and professional life had demonstrated this passion. It was the "lens" through which he viewed his entire life. It was present in his family, his relationships, *and* his work life. It was what he was really all about. He grew to understand that purpose was deeper and broader than his goals. It was the foundation on which he had built his life.

People in organizations are primarily looking for meaning in their work. But not many leaders act as though they believe that's what really motivates people. They think money motivates people. At the end of the day, people want to know they've done something meaningful.

—Bill George

PURPOSE IS BIGGER AND DEEPER THAN OUR GOALS

How often have you heard someone say about extraordinary people, "He was born to do this. She was born to do that." It is as if the "thing" was their only goal, their only reason for being. What happens when the "thing" is done or the career is over? Does that mean the person no longer has a purpose? Are these people then expendable to the Universe? *Purpose is life flowing through us.* Sometimes we may inhibit or ignore the flow, but it is always there seeking expression. How it manifests itself depends on our ability to open up to it and the particular circumstances we may be facing at the time. Purpose is constant. The manifestation of purpose is always changing.

I once had a client who asked me, "How can I tell the difference between obsessively or compulsively driven behavior and purposefully driven behavior? It is difficult to tell them apart sometimes." Purpose releases energy. The higher the purpose, the greater the energy. Purpose also frees us. The more profound the purpose, the greater the sense of freedom. Purpose opens up possibilities. Obsession or compulsion drains our energy and binds us to the activity itself.

Less joy, less energy, less freedom are the result. When observing the passionate, focused behavior of people, it can sometimes be difficult to know if the person is being obsessive or purposeful. If the behavior is adding energy, joy, and fulfillment to them and others, then it probably is coming from a purposeful place.

Take some time to observe your own behavior. Is it coming from a place of purpose? Is it releasing energy, or is it coming from a place of obligation, conditioning, duty, and bondage? Has your life become a series of "Have to do's" or is it moving in the direction of "Want to do's"? Take a few minutes and sketch out a "balance sheet" of "Have to do's" versus "Want to do's." How much *equity of purpose* is on your personal balance sheet? Are you living and leading the way you really want?

INSIGHTS • REFLECTIONS • COMMITMENTS •

Often the search for purpose in our own lives leads us to question the purpose of life itself. A story about a seeker of purpose illustrates this principle. For years a seeker was looking for his life's purpose. But each time he went deeply into his own being, the same question would surface within him: "If the Absolute Reality is omnipotent, omnipresent, the source of everything, why did it bother to create the universe in the first place?" After struggling with this question for quite some time, he eventually approached his spiritual teacher and posed the question. The response from the wise old master was direct and clear, "For the sake of purposeful play. All life is the purposeful play of the Creator." Ponder the implications of that for awhile: It is one of the most profound ideas I have ever heard.

So how are you doing in your own "playground"? Is your life full of purposeful play, or is it full of drudgery and work? We have all experienced times in our lives when work was more like play, and life proceeded in a type of frictionless flow. During such purposeful times, we are able to achieve extraordinary things with ease.

The world of ours has been constructed like a superbly written novel; we pursue the tale with avidity, hoping to discover the plot.

—Sir Arthur Keith

What gives your life that sense of purposeful play? The following reflective exercise may give you some clues.

REFLECTION

PURPOSE MASTERY

Discovering How We Express Our Gifts to Create Value

1. You have only two years to live and will do so with your normal energy and vitality. What will you do with these last two years?

2. I feel most energetic, fulfilled, and "full of life" when I . . .

3. You just won the $100 million lottery jackpot. What will you do with the rest of your life?

4. What is that "something more" inside you waiting for expression?

5. What is the recurring theme of your life—the "thing" you are always motivated to do—that is present in all your energetic, fulfilling moments?

6. My gifts are:

7. How are you expressing your gifts to make a difference as a leader?

8. How are you expressing your gifts to make a difference in all parts of your life?

CONNECTING THE INNER WITH THE OUTER: PURPOSE, AUTHENTICITY, AND CONGRUENCE

When we look at the lives of highly effective people, often there is a common theme. Their reason for being was clear to them. This connection, sense of meaning, love for what they do, often drove their success. When we are certain of our meaning and purpose, it is very difficult to keep us from achieving our objectives. Achievements come as natural by-products of our connection to our purpose.

> *Life ought to be a struggle of desire toward adventures whose nobility will fertilize the soul.*
>
> —Rebecca West

Start expanding your boundaries by giving yourself permission to pursue your dreams, passions, and goals. The keys to this pursuit may be closer than you think. The things that you regard as important surround you every day, although you may not regard them as "relevant." Open your eyes and observe how you spend your time—your purpose may be at hand:

• *Observe and Study People Whom You Admire*

We typically admire certain people not only because of their achievements, character, or personality, but because they connect with something *inside of us* which we regard as meaningful. Studying these people (whether historical or living) will help you to clarify the passions within you. Over the years, many of our clients have taken the initiative to contact people they admire. Most clients were surprised by how open these people were to sharing their life experiences. Such interactions can ignite our passion and serve as an impetus for a whole new career-life direction. Mastery of Purpose is not reserved for a few people. It is waiting for expression from within.

• *Look Closely at Your Hobbies, Reading, and Memberships*

Your hobbies, reading, and memberships are clues to your purpose. Look more deeply into them. Your purpose may be waiting! I once worked with a corporate financial executive whose passion for learning led him to create a wonderful position at a university—all because he first opened up to his core purpose.

• *Daydream*

Set aside practical concerns and try this: Sit in the backyard in the lawn chair and watch the clouds go by. What are some of your purposeful dreams? How do you see yourself living? How do you see yourself leading? Too often most of us dream and then "come back to reality." *Masterful people dream and then take purposeful action.*

So, what is your purpose, your reason for being? The answer to this will change your life. To achieve real success and fulfillment, ultimately we have to master purpose. Otherwise we may be achieving lots of *things* in life but not fully expressing our *purpose* in life. Purpose is the one achievement that is worth seeking with our entire heart and mind.

INSIGHTS • REFLECTIONS • COMMITMENTS •

EIGHT POINTS OF AWARENESS FOR LEADING BY EXPRESSING OUR GIFTS

Keep the following principles in mind as you get on the path to Mastery of Purpose.

1. Get in Touch with What Is Important to You: Values are the guideposts to purpose. Understanding what is important, what gives meaning to our life, is the compass to finding our purpose.

If you have trouble identifying what is really important to you, pay attention to what energizes and excites you, what expands your boundaries and brings you happiness. Explore what energizes and inspires you, and you will be on the pathway to purpose.

At various points in your life, you will face a vague sense that there must be something more, some deeper meaning. These are the times you need to dive deep into these experiences to uncover purpose seeking expression. At these moments, your purpose may be calling, but your lack of listening creates the "vagueness."

Purpose is the hope-filled glow of a meaningful life. It illuminates all circumstances of living.

—Cecile Burzynski

2. Act "On-Purpose": Most people have an intuitive sense about their purpose in life. Unfortunately, they treat it as a "dream" and never view it as "practical." Following your dream is the *most practical* thing you can possibly do with your life. But you have to have commitment. Commitment bridges your inner purpose to your outer action. David Prosser, Chairman of RTW, shared with me, "When your commitments are aligned with your purpose then great things will happen." Committing yourself to pursuing your purpose will marshal energies and potentialities within that you did not know you had.

The next time you are daydreaming in your lawn chair about what you really would like to do, get up from that lounger and take steps to achieve it! Every day, remind yourself what that "dream" felt like and every day commit to the practical steps to move toward it. When you face doubts that inhibit you from acting, doubt your doubts and trust your dreams.

3. Encourage Others to Find Purpose: Try supporting people around you by encouraging them to find their own purpose. Often times, the best support we can provide others is not solving their problems, but rather helping them to find their purpose. When people connect to meaning in their lives, many problems are eliminated or at least put into proper perspective. Remember, your purpose in life is probably not the same as their purpose. Encourage people to "get on their path," not to take your path or the path you think they should take!

4. Do Not Mistake the Path for the Goal: Be careful not to simply adopt other people's views as your purpose. Too often people externalize the latest personal development trend, spiritual teaching, or management guru theory into a dogmatic, inflexible, restrictive practice. This is mistaking the path for the goal. Finding your purpose is finding your essence or calling in life, not just adopting the belief systems of someone else. Personal development programs, religious systems, and great teachers are the paths, the techniques, not the goal. Be careful with programs or systems that impose beliefs onto you, thereby creating more dependency and externalization of the real you. If the process values your uniqueness, individuality, and personal path, it may be helpful. Always remind yourself that the program or practice (no matter how stimulating or fulfilling) is the technique— not the goal. The only genuine goal is inside you, and these processes are there to help you discover that.

INSIGHTS • REFLECTIONS • COMMITMENTS •

5. Focus on Service: Purpose always serves—it is the manner in which we use our gifts to make a difference in the world. Purpose is not purpose without adding value to others. It is not self-expression for its own sake; it is self-expression that creates value for those around you. Therefore, key into your gifts, but don't stop there. Focus on expressing your gifts to improve the lives of everyone and everything you touch.

6. Be Purposeful in All Domains: Too often we might be purposeful in one domain of our life and not another. We may be purposeful at work and not so much at home, or we may be purposeful in relationships but not in our work. Once you realize how your gifts can make a difference, then examine the degree to which you are being purposeful in all parts of your life. Seeing these purpose gaps can reveal our growth challenges. Too many purposeful leaders have lost their sense of purpose because they were not using their gifts in their personal lives, or because they were not expressing fully all aspects of themselves in their work. Congruence of purpose in all domains of our life is the goal of Purpose Mastery.

7. *Learn from "Failure":* Failure is a subjective label we apply to unintended or unexpected experiences. Usually, we are unwilling or unable to integrate these experiences into a meaningful context.

Every experience is a golden thread of meaning in our life's tapestry.

—Jody Thone Lande

From the vantage point of Purpose Mastery, failure does not exist. It is life attempting to teach us some new lessons or trying to point some new directions. As Warren Bennis wrote in *On Becoming a Leader*, "Everywhere you trip is where the treasure lies." But we have to be open as we "trip." The next time you are experiencing something you didn't intend or expect, ask yourself, "What am I supposed to be learning from this?" When we are living life on-purpose, every life experience helps us to solve the hieroglyphic of meaning. In the words of Emerson, "The world becomes a glass dictionary."

8. *Be Flexible:* Genuine insight into our purpose can be a recurring theme that connects divergent spheres of our life. Like an orchestra interpreting a symphony, the expression of our purpose will change. For instance, someone's real purpose in life may be to guide and to nurture others. At different stages of the life cycle, this will be expressed very differently—as a child, as a parent, as a professional person, and as a retired person. We need to be flexible, open to the process of expressing our internal sense of purpose in many different roles throughout life.

LEADERSHIP GROWTH COMMITMENTS

PURPOSE MASTERY

Reflect on the learnings that have surfaced as you read this chapter. Identify three leadership growth commitments to enhance your meaning and purpose. Then identify the potential obstacles, resources needed and signs or measures of success.

1. Key Learnings:

A. _____

B. _____

C. _____

2. Leadership Growth Commitments:

A. _____

B. _____

C. _____

3. Resources Needed:

A. _____

B. _____

C. _____

4. Potential Obstacles:

A. _____

B. _____

C. _____

5. Timeline and Measures of Success:

A. _____

B. _____

C. _____

PURPOSE MASTERY SUMMARY

• *Focus on How to Make a Difference:* Connect with purpose by understanding how your gifts can be of service to the world. Leadership is expressing your talents in the service of others.

• *Get in Touch with Your Values:* Values will guide you to your purpose. Pay attention to what interests, energizes, and excites you. The language of leadership is expressed through our values; leaders remind people which values are important.

• *Act "On-Purpose":* Dream it and then do it! Doubt your doubts and remember your dreams. Courageous leaders are centered in purpose.

• *Be Purposeful in All Domains:* Understand your purpose gaps— those parts of your life lacking expression of purpose. Expand your purpose into all areas of your life.

• *Encourage Others to Find Purpose:* Be a true leader by helping others connect with what is meaningful to them.

• *Seek the Goal:* Be careful not to mistake the path for the goal. Seek your own unique purpose. The philosophies, techniques, or views of others are your tools, not your goal. Express your own leadership voice.

• *Learn from "Failure":* Be open to the purposeful learning contained in unexpected or unintended life experiences. The truest test of your character as a leader is the manner in which you deal with failure.

• *Be Flexible:* Even though your essential purpose will be a constant throughout your life, how you express it will change as you evolve through various stages.

PATHWAY THREE: CHANGE MASTERY

Leading in the Flow

Change Mastery involves embracing the purposeful learning
contained in the unending, creative flow of life.

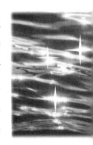

The north shore of Lake Superior is really an awesome sight. It's an inland sea unlike any other—the largest body of fresh water in the world. Cool, fresh pine scents the air. Black, rocky cliffs form an imposing backdrop as they disappear into the water's edge. Waterfalls tumble down rivers rushing to their destinations. As calming and refreshing as Superior is, she also is dangerously unpredictable. At a moment's notice, her calm temperament can become a raging force, swallowing huge ships whenever she pleases. Remember Gordon Lightfoot's song about the *Edmund Fitzgerald*? The *Edmund Fitzgerald* was one of her victims.

Growing up in Minnesota, I received adults' counsel about the Great Lake at a young age: "You can only survive the cold water of Superior for four or five minutes." In the spirit of adventure (some might say the spirit of foolishness), I decided to swim the lake.

Donning my wet suit (I'm not completely crazy), I entered the water. As I dove in, the cold water overwhelmed me. It felt breathtakingly, bone-achingly cold. In the first couple of minutes, I believed all the advice of my upbringing. I was sure I could not handle the cold. Then the water in my wet suit started to warm up and everything changed. I became intensely aware of being the only human in this huge mass of water. As I swam near the shore, I closely watched the crystal clear water with spears of light passing through it. When I swam further into its depth, the blackness of unbelievably deep drop-offs appeared and revealed the lake's immensity. After a short distance, new underwater cliffs and rock formations came into view. Swimming from point to point, I met with an odd mix of emotions. Ecstatic one moment and fearful the next, I felt all my emotions were possible and heightened as I explored this uncharted experience.

The cold water kept my heart rate so slow I could go on and on without difficulty. As I progressed, I had the distinct sensation that the lake was choosing to be cooperative with me—its new visitor. If she tired of my adventure, I would be history. I was immersed in the body of this entity, and she was accepting that (for the moment). After about three quarters of a mile down the coast, I decided not to overstay my welcome, and I turned back. As I feared it might, the lake grew impatient. Her waves, which moments ago swelled gently, now rolled harshly and threateningly. Because of the steep cliffs along the shoreline, there was no exit. An enjoyable swim was becoming a dangerous situation. All I could do was stay relaxed, tolerate the turbulent, changing waters, and keep my destination in sight. Fortunately I reached the shore when I did, which was only minutes before the lake decided to "wake up." Feeling at once exhilarated and thankful, I walked up the cliffs and passed an old-timer staring at me in disbelief. Irritatedly, he snarled, "You know, a fella could get killed doing that!" He was clearly astonished when I responded, "I know. But isn't life wonderful?"

> *We all live in suspense, from day to day, from hour to hour; in other words, we are the hero of our own story.*
>
> —Mary McCarthy

UNCOVERING THE LEARNING AND GROWTH CONTAINED IN CHANGE

Our lives are much like swimming in Superior. We dive into them, and we never really know what is going to happen next. We operate under the illusion that life remains constant, but in reality everything is always changing. From breath to breath, we exchange so many atoms we change the makeup of our physiology in a moment. In the course of one year, 98 percent of all our atoms are exchanged for new ones; we are literally *new people* each year. Our lives are an endless flow of change.

Although it may be true that we can't step into the same river twice, as Heraclitis once said, once we step in, we are part of that river's flow. Since birth, we have been swept up in a raging, constantly changing, never-ending flow of experience. Some people love the flow of life; others hate it and resist it. But, because the flow of the river is a constant, we have no choice in the matter. We have to change. It is part of the price of admission to life. Every moment our atoms are changing; our thoughts are changing; our emotions are changing; our relationships, our finances—change is endless and constant. We have no choice in the matter except for one aspect of change—mastering our ability to *adapt* to change.

Always struggling against the flow, we can constantly curse the fact that we have fallen into this river. Or we can enjoy the flow, accept it, trust it, and gently steer our way along as rapids appear, logs pass by, and placid pools arise. We can adapt to it, cooperate with it, and potentially influence its future direction. However, we cannot control it. Attempts to do so only lead to frustration, pain, and suffering. The joy of life comes from accepting the reality and thrill of the unknown. As the Zen Master Ekon wrote, "Who shall halt the swan in its flight, or life in its flow?"

Learning to be open to the purposeful learning contained in all change is no small task. Quite often we are dragged "kicking and screaming" to every lesson. As my colleague, Janet Feldman, likes to say, "People change more often because they *feel the heat* than because they *see the light*."

Glenn, a senior executive in a fast-growth, medium-size company, was about to feel the heat. He was extremely bright, with a Ph.D. in a technical discipline. His intellectual

INSIGHTS • REFLECTIONS • COMMITMENTS •

prowess was exceptional, but his emotional-interpersonal skills were not as highly developed. As he advanced through the growing organization, these liabilities became more prominent. Unfortunately, Glenn never really comprehended the importance of developing these inner resources. Despite honest feedback, professional assessment, and coaching, he just wasn't ready to grow. Because he didn't *see the light*, the heat overcame him and he was terminated.

Changes [in life] are not only possible and predictable, but to deny them is to be an accomplice to one's own unnecessary vegetation.

—Gail Sheehy

Glenn had never "failed" at anything in his life; the shock of this change was dramatic. For the first time, he was truly vulnerable. As William Bridges would have described it in his insightful writing on change, Glenn was "between the ending and the new beginning"—he was in the "journey through the wilderness." Fortunately, Glenn took full advantage of the creativity and developmental growth available in this "wilderness." He was finally ready to listen to coaching regarding his style and personality. For the first time, he committed to an action plan to transform his leadership approaches. Within months, he purchased his own business and created a new life. He succeeded because he was open to the purposeful learning contained in the change process.

Jim was a tough, crusty executive from the "old school." He was extremely bright and got exceptional results, but he also "bore holes" right through people in his drive for excellence. If someone didn't meet his expectations, he would rant and rave. Fewer and fewer people wanted to work with him, and it was starting to limit his career progression. When he was referred to us for executive coaching, I wasn't hopeful. I knew his reputation and doubted he was open to change. After several sessions at our *Executive to Leader Institute*, he was rapidly peeling away layers of self-understanding. To my surprise he was eagerly open to growth. He didn't intend to impact people negatively. He just didn't know how to get results differently. Years of parental modeling combined with a history of patterning himself after an extremely demanding, insecure boss had set his conditioning in place. Underneath the surface was a caring, sensitive, character-driven person. His family life and personal life were clear evidence of his inner being. Once he found congruence between his inner life and outer life, he evolved as a leader. Although he remained uncompromising on results, he transformed the way he got them. Why was he able to change? He was able to change because he was able to grow in a way that was consistent with his real nature. Change is dramatic and lasting when it is a purposeful growth toward who we really are.

BREAKING OLD PATTERNS AND OPENING UP TO CHANGE

Positive change requires letting go of old patterns and taking a fresh approach. It demands going beyond our pre-conceived ideas. A story about the relationship of a teacher and student illustrates this principle. A student who thought he had it "all figured out" would visit his teacher each day for personal lessons about life. Despite the teacher's attempts to share her life experience, the student always resisted. One day the teacher took a different approach. When he arrived, the teacher asked the student if he would like some tea. The teacher then proceeded to set the tea table and brought in a huge pot of piping hot tea. She not only filled the student's cup, but once the cup was full, she continued to pour. Tea overflowed. Covering the table and streaming onto the beautiful carpet, the hot tea ruined everything! The student was shocked. He jumped up from his chair and started screaming at the teacher, "Stop! You must be crazy! You're ruining everything! Can't you see what you are doing?" The teacher continued her pour-

INSIGHTS • REFLECTIONS • COMMITMENTS •

ing as if the student wasn't present until the entire pitcher was empty. Only then did she look calmly at the student and respond, "If you want to receive *my* tea, you must keep *your* cup empty."

Like a wise student, we can gain insight only if we are open to it. How often have you taken a detour in traffic and discovered a new, better route? Perhaps you have lost a job or relationship, only to connect with a better situation later? How many times has your once-favorite restaurant closed and you dis-covered a wonderful, new restaurant to replace it? How many difficult or unpleasant experi-ences end up being the most instructive? Change is always our teacher, pointing new directions, suggesting new options, testing our potentialities. *Change challenges our current reality by allowing a new reality to rush in*. If we're open to it, if our cup is empty, new possibilities flow into our lives. If we're not open to change, we respond to it like an enemy we have to fend off.

> *Change is the timeless interplay of the forces of creation and destruction.*
>
> —Janet Feldman

Unfortunately, resistance is a losing battle, because change is a relentless oppo-nent. When we resist change, what is the hidden dynamic? We usually are attempting to defend ourselves from the fear of loss. We fear that we will not survive the change without something familiar being lost. This is a truly accu-rate perception. We will lose something. However, we also are going to gain something. It may be something better, if we are open to the purposeful learn-ing present.

One of the most lucid descriptions of how the change process feels comes from Danaan Parry in *Warriors of the Heart*:

> Sometimes I feel that my life is a series of trapeze swings. I'm either hanging on to a trapeze bar swinging along or, for a few moments in my life, I'm hurtling across space in between trapeze bars.
>
> Most of the time, I spend my life hanging on for dear life to my trapeze-bar-of-the-moment. It carries me along at a certain steady rate of swing, and I have the feeling that I'm in control of my life. I

know most of the right questions and even some of the right answers. But once in a while, as I'm merrily (or not-so-merrily) swinging along, I look out ahead of me into the distance, and what do I see? I see another trapeze bar swing towards me. It's empty, and I know, in that place in me that knows, that this new trapeze bar has my name on it. It is my next step, my growth, my aliveness coming to get me. In my heart-of-hearts, I know that for me to grow, I must release my grip on this present, well-known bar to move to the new one.

Every time it happens to me, I hope that I won't have to grab the new bar. But in my knowing place I know that I must totally release my grasp on my old bar, and for some moment in time, I must hurdle across space before I can grab onto the new bar. Each time I am filled with terror. It doesn't matter that in all my previous hurdles across the void of unknowing, I have always made it. Each time I am afraid that I will miss, that I will be crushed on unseen rocks in the bottomless chasm between the bars. But I do it anyway. Perhaps this is the essence of what the mystics call the faith experience. No guarantees, no net, no insurance policies, but you do it anyway because somehow, to keep hanging on to that old bar is no longer on the list of alternatives. And so for an eternity that can last a microsecond or a thousand lifetimes, I soar across the dark void of "the past is gone; the future is not yet here." It's called transition. I have come to believe that is the only place that real change occurs. I mean real change, not the pseudo-change that only lasts until the next time my old buttons get punched.

INSIGHTS • REFLECTIONS
• COMMITMENTS •

So, if change is so great, why do we fear it? We fear it because change always involves both creation and destruction. As something new is created, something old is destroyed. The bud is destroyed as the flower blooms. The caterpillar is destroyed as the butterfly ascends. Our inhibition comes as we face the prospect of replacing the familiar with the unknown. At the junction of those two realities, most of us retreat. Usually it is only after change is thrust upon us that we accept it because we often realize our lives actually will be better.

In order to be utterly happy, the only thing necessary is to refrain from comparing this moment with other moments in the past, which I often did not fully enjoy because I was comparing them with other moments of the future.

—André Gide

DEVELOPING PRESENT-MOMENT AWARENESS TO DEAL WITH CHANGE EFFECTIVELY

Even though the only "place" we can handle change is in the present, most of us live our lives in the past or the future. Until we learn to live our lives in the flow of the present, we can never really deal with change effectively. At the most fundamental level of our lives, there is only the present moment. When we worry about keeping things like they were in the past and avoiding some new, unknown future, we limit our ability to impact our success in the present. If our awareness is cluttered by the "static" of the past and future, we can never focus deeply on the *now*. As a result, we can never perform to the height of our abilities, particularly in the midst of dynamic change. We need to become now-focused like a professional athlete with single-minded devotion to a task in the midst of very dynamic circumstances. As we build our focus in the present, we begin to gain confidence that we can handle the *endless chain of present moments* throughout our lives. Change Mastery is about developing an unshakable inner confidence that we can handle and can learn from whatever comes our way. It's an inner confidence that we can deal with real change—unexpected change—not just the run-of-the-mill type of anticipated change.

Learning to cultivate this centered, present-moment awareness takes practice on a day-to-day level. We can begin with mundane levels of change and then build our change capacity to higher, more dynamic levels much like an athlete in training. Several months ago, I was returning from a conference in New York City. Like most conferences, it was a combination of some learning, some inspiration, some good speakers, some bad speakers, not enough sleep, and some lousy food. Needless to say, I was ready to return home. My flight back to Minneapolis went smoothly. I arrived at the gate fifteen minutes early, my baggage was the first off the plane, and everything went like clockwork. I had "found time" on my hands. My business partner, Cecile Burzynski, and I had agreed that she would pick me up at the airport after her appointment at a corporate client's offices nearby. We would have lunch and catch up with one another and the business. So I went to the curb and waited. What was I going to do with so much found time in my life—a luxury I rarely experience?

As I waited near the passenger pick-up I could still feel the buzz of New York City in my head, and I could sense the same type of on-edge energy around me. Every person waiting to be picked up seemed to be in an irritable mood. One guy repeatedly pounded his fist on the trunk of an arriving car so his spouse would open the trunk latch. Another, with his portable phone plastered to his cheek, hurled his bags into the back seat and began shouting orders to his business associate. As I was observing the scene I said to myself, "This is no way to live. I'm going to make sure Cecile feels appreciated when she gets here. I'm going to wait patiently."

Maintaining this attitude was fairly easy for the first half hour; after all, I had arrived early and had gained a half hour in my life. But when the second half hour began, I was

INSIGHTS • REFLECTIONS • COMMITMENTS •

starting to feel those primordial "time is of the essence" rumblings. Catching myself regressing toward the early stages of behavioral evolution demonstrated by my "curb mates," I affirmed, "I don't care if it takes an hour, I'm going to be pleasant to Cecile, and in the meantime I'm going to extract whatever learning I can from the present moment." As an entrepreneur and strategist, I frequently live my life in the future. I am thinking of the next new product we'll design, the next presentation I'll make, or the next client I'll meet. At

Trust is our trail guide through the wilderness of change.

—Bill McCarthy

that moment, I truly became aware of what it was like to be in the present. My commitment was so complete, it changed my perception of the entire situation. Letting go of my rigid time focus and my tendency to focus always on the future, I started to notice new things in

the present. The air was fresh, crisp, clear. I started to notice how excited the children (and dogs) in the approaching cars were as they came to pick up moms, dads, grandmas and grandpas, aunts and uncles. Even though the people they were picking up were sometimes grumpy, it didn't matter to the kids or animals—they were in the joy of the present. I started to feel good; I started to unwind and relax. I was dealing with change on an everyday level.

Fortunately, Cecile arrived only a half hour late. Her client meeting had run slightly longer, and midday traffic had been a bit snarled. So, in keeping with my commitment, I approached her car with a buoyant attitude and gave her a warm greeting and "thanks" before she had the chance to apologize for running late. As we headed to a nearby restaurant for lunch, she asked me how the flight was. I said with all sincerity, "The flight was fine, but the last hour of waiting was *really* terrific. I got some great insights about being present." Her eyes widened as she glanced quickly away from merging traffic and with a tongue-in-cheek attitude said, "We need to get you back to the office. You're taking Change Mastery much too seriously!"

How often does our inability to master these everyday situations cause unnecessary stress, tension, loss of productivity, and ineffective relationships? The ability to cope with large and small changes not only improves the quality of our lives, it greatly enhances our effectiveness.

Bridging the Paradox of Immediate Focus and Broad Awareness for Leading During Turbulent Times

The most effective people I've coached over the years have been able to straddle an important paradox. They not only could sustain a sharp, localized focus in the present moment, but at the same time could maintain a broad, purposeful context. Being able to maintain a sharp focus and broad comprehension simultaneously is one of the most important qualities for both leadership effectiveness and dealing with change. It reminds me of how I felt in Lake Superior as the waves were kicking up. In order to cope, I had to relax and focus on the quality of my swim stroke while at the same time I kept the goal clearly in mind. Too much attention on one or the other, and the results could have been disastrous. Effective people can bridge these two realities as they navigate through change. Admittedly, doing so can be a real challenge when dramatic, unexpected change brings us to our knees.

Walter was a human resource executive for a financial institution. His career had been a steady progression through the organization. He wasn't flashy. He was solid, reliable, responsible, and got results. He had been loyal to the organization and was totally dedicated to it. When the organizational dynamics rapidly shifted, he didn't fit anymore; he was totally shocked and devastated. Walter conducted a long, tough, job search, which took its toll on him and his finances. Eventually he found a new job and sat down with me to celebrate. To my surprise, he couldn't say a word; all he could do was sob deeply and gasp for air. I knew he was happy,

INSIGHTS • REFLECTIONS • COMMITMENTS •

but this was extreme. Once composed he said, "Kevin, I probably should have told you this before, but I was so ashamed. I almost took my life two months ago. I went into my garage, sealed off all the doors and cracks, and turned on my car. As I sat there intending to end it all, I remembered your advice—focus on what's important to you and where you want to end up, no matter how difficult things seem. I thought of my daughter and everything I still wanted to do with my life. I flew out of the car and got into the fresh air just in time. I'm so emotional today because I know I didn't just get a job, I got my life." I am always inspired by these reminders of how our purpose and values are the rudders which help us to navigate through the raging whitewater of change.

> *The opposite of trusting in the unexpected is trying to control the uncontrollable— clearly an impossible task.*
>
> —Angeles Arrien

LEARNING TO TRUST OURSELVES AMID DYNAMIC CHANGE

Sometimes even our purpose and values aren't enough to get us through change. At times things are moving so rapidly, all we can do is *trust*. Last year, I was driving about fifty miles per hour in a rainstorm on an interstate highway. As I drove through this blinding rain, I was listening to an audiotape about trusting yourself during times of change. Little did I know how relevant the tape was going to be. A moment later, I heard something hit my roof and realized my fancy, long windshield wiper (my one and only wiper blade) on my fancy new car had flown right over the top of my vehicle. I couldn't see a thing. Naturally, at first I started to panic; then I heard this reassuring voice on the tape encouraging me to trust myself. So I did. I trusted my intuition and navigated my way off the freeway. I'm still amazed that I didn't crash. When I got back to the office, I told a colleague about what had happened and my amazing "trust experience." She advised, *"Trust me*, get rid of that stupid car!" In times of rapid change, trusting ourselves and our intuition may be our only guide. If that doesn't work, at least buy a car with two wiper blades.

In the business world, maintaining trust through the tough times can be very challenging—particularly when coming face-to-face with failure. At the Toro Company, trust is the bridge to a "freedom-to-fail" environment. Rather than shooting down the teams whose ideas don't work, Toro trusts its people enough to celebrate the "failures." Ken Melrose, CEO of Toro, shared with me a real-life story of a Toro team that failed in its attempt to save the company time and money by making a new metal hood for a riding lawn mower. Unfortunately, after considerable investment, the project failed. A short time later, Ken called the team to his office. As they gathered outside, they feared the worst. As they entered Ken's office, they were completely surprised to be greeted by a celebration with balloons and refreshments. Ken shared with them, "Most innovative ideas don't work out. We need to keep trusting, creating, risking, and celebrating the good 'tries'— particularly when things don't work out."

INSIGHTS • REFLECTIONS • COMMITMENTS •

LEADERSHIP DEVELOPMENT AS MEASURED BY OUR ABILITY TO ADAPT

Adaptability is another crucial quality for effectively dealing with change. I'm sure it's not an exaggeration to say that our personal and professional effectiveness is in direct proportion to our ability to adapt to change. Even the evolution of our species can be measured by its resilient ability to adapt. In *The Guardian,* Buckminster Fuller wrote, "Everyone is too specialized now. We couldn't be getting ourselves into worse trouble since we know that biological species become extinct because they over-specialize and fail to adapt. Society is all tied up with specialization. If nature had wanted you to be a specialist, she'd have had you born with one eye and with a microscope attached to it."

Many people live like they are observing life through the fixed gaze of a microscope. The most fatal obstacle to an effective life is a

fixed, unyielding point of view. If we view life in a single-dimensional manner, we will always be disappointed and frustrated. With such a rigid, fixed
view, life will never "live up" to our limited definitions. Our lives eventually
will be shattered at the first unexpected experience. Since life is growth and
motion, a fixed, inflexible view is our greatest threat to an effective life. As
Arnold Toynbee said in *Cities on the Move*, "The quality in human nature on
which we must pin our hopes is its proven adaptability." If we hope to be more
effective leaders, we must pin our hopes on our ability to deal with all life
throws at us by changing, adapting, and growing.

*Man never made any
material as resilient as the
human spirit.*

—Ben Williams

The *Tao Te Ching* captured the essence of
Change Mastery: "Whatever is flexible and
flowing will tend to grow; whatever is rigid
and blocked will wither and die." I'm quite
certain that Lao Tzu was referring not only to
people and natural systems, but to organiza-
tional structures as well. This concept has become more clear to me over the
years as I have witnessed firsthand organizations that are "flowing" and those
that are "blocked." However, getting the flow going on an organizational level
is a very challenging proposition. Individuals can wake up to their potential
rapidly; organizations awaken more slowly. While some organizations simply
are rearranging the deck chairs on the Titanic, others are genuinely re-thinking
the concept of "the ship" altogether.

It is encouraging to see that some organizations are not merely treating reengineering as a management guru theory but as an all-encompassing process from
top to bottom. However, a parallel reengineering process is required to ensure
success—the "reengineering" of human development processes. It is crucial to
give people the development tools they need. With them, they will unfold and
re-think their true potentialities as they connect them to a changing organization. Organizations that are looking at process improvement, reengineering,
and quality as a total organizational *and* human development system will
thrive in change. At Deluxe Corporation, they call it the "Deluxe Way," a massive remobilization and retooling of their human capital to be a sustainable,

high performance, 21st-century company. Led by CEO Gus Blanchard, the investment required to achieve the Deluxe Way is no small line item. Blanchard views the human capital investment this way: "This can't just be talk. We need to invest millions of dollars in people development and keep with it even if we experience a few bumps in the road, just like you would stick to your commitments in product development or R&D." The courage to reengineer the total organization (human and systemic) comes from the belief that people really are the capital that drives performance.

DEVELOPING THE RESILIENCE TO THRIVE IN CHANGE

INSIGHTS • REFLECTIONS • COMMITMENTS •

Unfortunately, many leaders excel at *talking about* reengineering and change. Change is usually seen as something happening "out there": The world changes, products change, competition changes, systems and processes change, technology changes. While I was coaching a CEO on a major change initiative, he hesitantly said to me, "Let me get this straight: You mean to say that *I'm* going to have to change?" All significant change begins with self-change. Reengineering begins with oneself. As Peter Block writes in *Stewardship*, "If there is no transformation inside each of us, all the structural change in the world will have no impact on our institution."

Moving our concept of change from an outside-in paradigm to an inside-out paradigm has profound implications. When viewed from this perspective, we see change as an internal dynamic—an internal process of learning and development. Change is perceived as something to be mastered from within versus something going on outside of us. Ultimately, people resist, adapt, or learn from it. In this regard, all change fundamentally takes place within the person. In his book, *Servant Leadership*, Robert Greenleaf expresses it like this: "To the servant leader, the process of change starts in here, in the servant, not out there."

David Prosser, chairman of the fast-growing public company RTW, shared with me how he "re-invented himself": "Twelve years ago, I was 60 years old,

Experience is not what happens to a man; it is what a man does with what happens to him.

—Aldous Huxley

and by all external measures I was very successful. I was standing outside my lake home in suburban Minneapolis, and I happened to notice my huge home with my big Mercedes parked in front. In a moment, it dawned on me that despite all this external stuff and success, I wasn't happy. I knew then and there that I needed to transform myself to transform my life. Over the next few years, I committed myself to personal growth. My personal work culminated in the realization that I wanted to serve people by making a difference in the world. This reinvention of myself eventually led me to found RTW, which is committed to transforming the Workers Compensation system in the United States. If you want to change the world, start by changing yourself—then go out and change the world."

As we have helped leaders to deal more effectively with change from within, we have observed *Five Change Mastery Shifts* required to enhance performance:

- *Change Mastery Shift #1: From Problem Focus to Opportunity Focus.* Effective leaders tend to perceive and to focus on the opportunities inherent in change.

- *Change Mastery Shift #2: From Short-Term Focus to Long-Term Focus.* Effective leaders don't lose sight of their long-term vision in the midst of change.

- *Change Mastery Shift #3: From Circumstance Focus to Purpose Focus.* Effective leaders maintain a clear purpose regardless of immediate circumstances.

- *Change Mastery Shift #4: From Control Focus to Adaptability Focus.* Effective leaders understand constant control is not possible, but adaptability allows them and others to flow with change.

- *Change Mastery Shift #5: From Doubt Focus to Trust Focus.* Effective leaders are more secure in themselves; they possess a sense that they can handle whatever may come their way.

Let's take some time to bring all of this closer to home. Use the following questions to reflect on how you deal with change in your life.

INSIGHTS • REFLECTIONS • COMMITMENTS •

REFLECTION

CHANGE MASTERY

*Uncovering Personal Learning from
Our Change Experiences*

1. Think about the times you faced major crises or challenges. What qualities or potentialities arose? What qualities would you like to develop further during those times of crisis? What were the key things you learned during those times?

2. When presented with a new experience, what is your first reaction?

3. How do you react when you have invested significant work and effort into something and it doesn't work out?

4. What do you fear most?

5. The next time you face a potential loss, how will you cope differently?

6. Reflect on how well you:

    Focus on Opportunities vs. Problems

    Focus on Long Term vs. Short Term

    Focus on Purpose vs. Circumstance

    Focus on Adaptability vs. Control

    Focus on Trust vs. Doubt

Measuring Our Ability to Deal with Change

Managing change is a hot topic today. Leaders at all levels of the organization are being challenged to perform like no other time in business history. How well do we prepare our talent to be up to the task? Certainly most of the training in change management, process improvement, and reengineering is valuable. But are we really preparing leaders and all employees to thrive in change? Are we helping people to develop the inner resilience required, or are we throwing them into the lion's den of change and hoping they will somehow survive?

With the rapid change in our information age, the old-world "survival of the fittest" mentality is rapidly becoming obsolete. The whole idea of "fittest" needs to be redefined. No longer a measure of physical prowess or power, it needs to be re-thought in terms of survival of the most aware or survival of the most flexible—mentally, emotionally, and spiritually. The emerging paradigm for success in the coming years will convert from the concept of external exertion to one of inner mastery. Survival of the most aware is becoming the true underlying foundation for lasting effectiveness. Are we gaining mastery from the inside out to withstand the tumult of change, or are we reacting and defending ourselves against every change that comes our way? Are we caught in an endless cycle of fear?

If our fear of loss exceeds our personal coping strategies, we will be overwhelmed, and therefore ineffective, in dealing with change. It all boils down to unfolding the coping resources within us. Imagine how

INSIGHTS • REFLECTIONS
• COMMITMENTS •

bold and wonderful our lives would be if our purpose, vision, and resilience were so strong that fear would not have a hold over us. Outstanding leaders like Franklin Delano Roosevelt understood this dynamic: "We have nothing to fear but fear itself." These words are spoken from a place of true character—a place of unshakable inner conviction, strength, and awareness. They are not merely a cleverly crafted phrase but an expression of a deep, internally driven leader. Imagine your life totally free of fear. You would harbor no financial fear, no fear of failure, no fear of loss—no fear whatsoever. How would you live? How would you lead?

When nothing is sure, everything is possible.

—Margaret Drabble

SEVEN POINTS OF AWARENESS FOR LEADING IN THE FLOW OF CHANGE

As you develop Change Mastery, keep the following principles in mind:

1. Be Open to the Learning: When we resist change, all our energy is bound up in the effort to maintain the status quo. In this restricted state of awareness, we miss the lessons trying to be delivered to us. There's no need to deny the challenges you are experiencing. Encourage yourself to open up consciously to the learning hidden in the changing circumstances. Grow with the flow.

2. Practice Present-Moment Awareness: In the midst of change, we often cope by escaping mentally and emotionally to the past or future. As a result, we rarely live in the present. Imagine a tennis player preoccupied with her past matches or potential future matches in the midst of a dynamic set. Would she be successful? Developing focus in the present moment allows us to begin to "connect up" a series of present-moment successes into a lifetime of effectiveness. Think about it: *Isn't the present moment our only opportunity to influence the course of our lives?*

3. Integrate Immediate Focus and Broad Awareness: It may sound like a paradox, but highly effective people have learned to integrate a localized focus with comprehensive awareness. They zero in on the present moment without losing the broader sense of their vision and purpose. Being deeply focused yet simultaneously aware of the meaningful context of our lives is one of the keys to inside-out success. Many successful people describe their broad, purposeful awareness to be like a screen on which all the focused, localized events of their lives are connected in a meaningful way.

4. Trust Yourself: Sometimes the "G-forces" of change are so intense, all we can do is sit back, hold on, and trust that everything will work out. Developing our inner ability to trust is crucial as we hurl through the air between our trapeze bars. As André Gide wrote, "One does not discover new lands without consenting to lose sight of the shore for a very long time."

INSIGHTS • REFLECTIONS • COMMITMENTS •

5. Develop Resiliency Through Mental-Emotional Stretching: Our current state of development or personal evolution can be measured directly by our *ability to adapt.* Our life shrinks and expands in proportion to our personal flexibility. To "limber up," start to stretch yourself in the mundane, everyday events of life. How are you adapting to the slow traffic? How are you reacting to being late for an important presentation or being open to someone else's "unusual" style or background? What is your response to trying something new? Gradually increase your emotional-mental-spiritual flexibility to prepare yourself for life's major events. Follow the same principles used for physical training: stretch, don't strain—micro-millimeters of daily progress are sufficient. As we regularly practice this type of training, our elasticity may be experienced as a calm and centered sense of self in the midst of unpredictable events. As resiliency unfolds, we begin to have an inner sense that we can handle whatever comes our way. Follow the advice of Benjamin Franklin, "Be not disturbed at trifles or at accidents, common or unavoidable."

*6. **Practice the Change Mastery Shifts:*** To deal with change as a leader, constantly challenge yourself to make the five Change Mastery Shifts:

They must often change who would be constant in happiness or wisdom.

—Confucius

- Move from problem focus to opportunity focus.
- Move from short-term focus to long-term focus.
- Move from circumstance focus to purpose focus.
- Move from control focus to adaptability focus.
- Move from doubt focus to trust focus.

Making these shifts will transform your leadership effectiveness by shifting from being persona-driven to being character-driven.

*7. **Take the Leap:*** Accept the fact that you will always feel some hesitation and anxiety when facing the trapeze bar. Learning to see beyond the fear of loss and into purpose and vision gives us the courage to take the leap. I like to tell people as they are facing the "trapeze bar" of the moment, "Hey, Buddy, can you dare some change?" When faced with the prospect of change, think of the bold inner confidence expressed in this Zen poem:

> Ride your horse along the edge of the sword,
> Hide yourself in the middle of the flames,
> Blossoms of the fruit tree bloom in the fire,
> The sun rises in the evening.

LEADERSHIP GROWTH COMMITMENTS

CHANGE MASTERY

Reflect on the learnings that have surfaced as you read this chapter. Identify three leadership growth commitments to enhance your ability to thrive in change. Then identify the potential obstacles, resources needed, and signs or measures of success.

1. Key Learnings:
A. _____
B. _____
C. _____

2. Leadership Growth Commitments:
A. _____
B. _____
C. _____

3. Resources Needed:
A. _____
B. _____
C. _____

4. Potential Obstacles:
A. _____
B. _____
C. _____

5. Timeline and Measures of Success:
A. _____
B. _____
C. _____

CHANGE MASTERY SUMMARY

- *Be Open to Learning:* Instead of spending your energy resisting change, look for the growth and learning contained within the flow of change. The learning leader outperforms the learned leader every time.

- *Practice Present-Moment Awareness:* Success can be created only in the present. Learn to focus deeply in the present moment to weave a series of present-moment successes into a lifetime of achievement. Leaders balance their vision with an acute awareness of the opportunities and learning available in the present.

- *Integrate Immediate Focus and Broad Awareness:* Bridge the paradox of being fully present without losing your broader purpose and vision. Leadership requires a localized focus painted onto a broader, meaningful canvas.

- *Trust Yourself:* As the pace of change intensifies, your inner sense of trust may be the only bridge you have to straddle the leadership gulf between the known and unknown. Trust bridges the leader to his or her vision.

- *Develop Resiliency Through Mental-Emotional Stretching:* Your life expands or contracts in relation to your personal flexibility. Stretching yourself in mundane circumstances builds up your elasticity to handle major life and leadership challenges.

- *Practice the Change Mastery Shifts:* Build awareness of the Change Mastery Shifts to move from being a persona-driven leader to being a character-driven leader.

- *Take the Leap:* In those fortunate moments of being able to choose change, step back; if the choice connects to your values and purpose, take the leap. Leadership is the purposeful leap into the future.

PATHWAY FOUR: INTERPERSONAL MASTERY

Leading Through Synergy

*Interpersonal Mastery is the dynamic blending of personal
power with synergy power to create value and contribution.*

Martin was an incredibly gifted executive; his talent and intelligence were apparent
in everything he did. At early stages of his career his cognitive and intellectual skills
helped him to excel in many challenging, complex assignments around the
globe. As his achievements advanced, Martin started to believe "his press" and
internalized the belief that "he was the person who made things happen at his
organization." He began to lose touch with the synergy that was supporting his
accomplishments. He thought he was the prime mover, and in reality his teams
were the ones creating and supporting his achievements. Gradually his relationships started to become strained, and he couldn't understand why. To help him
break through his self-limiting view, we asked him to outline each key event in
his life over the past two weeks by focusing on the people that made each event
possible. It didn't take him long to recognize the web of interdependence that
was *supporting his success*. He became aware of initiatives for which he had taken
credit and for which he now needed to acknowledge others. He was beginning
to bridge personal power with synergy power to enhance his contribution.

In a recent study of 6,403 middle and upper managers conducted by the
Foundation for Future Leadership, men and women received their *highest* eval-
uations for their intellectual competencies. Both groups also received their *lowest*
marks for their interpersonal competencies. Although women did score higher
than men in communication skills overall, the relative trends were the same.
Both groups were highest in their intellectual and their control skills and lowest
in their interpersonal skills. This study validates precisely what we've seen in

coaching leaders over the past 20 years—leaders must expand their competencies from simply getting results to adding value through synergy.

BUILDING RELATIONSHIP BRIDGES

Relationships are the bridges that connect authentic self-expression to creating value. Leadership is *not* self-expression for its own sake; it's self-expression that makes a difference, that enriches the lives of others. Leadership does not exist in a vacuum—it always operates in context, in relationships. While leaders may lead by virtue of who they are, leaders also create value by virtue of their relationships. As the chairman of a technology services firm shared with me, "Leadership is not about sitting in your office and dreaming up strategy—it is about touching the organization through personal presence and relationship."

> *To build enlightening relationships, we have to develop the skill of setting intentions that simultaneously serve our own evolution and the growth of the relationship.*
>
> —Gay and Kathlyn Hendricks

As crucial as relationships are to leadership success, many leaders have a difficult time breaking out of the self-limiting illusion that they are "the ones that make things happen." All too often, successful, achievement-oriented people mistakenly believe they are the prime movers, the origin of accomplishments in their groups or organizations. Most leaders would not admit to this, but often their behavior clearly demonstrates this tendency. Unfortunately, many driven leaders fail to comprehend how nothing is accomplished without engaging in relationships and appreciating the unique contribution of many, many people. Some leaders even feel slowed down or frustrated by the teaming or synergy process. Lawrence Perlman, Chairman and CEO of Ceridian, sees it differently: "Leadership will not add enough value if it only comes from the top—it needs to come from the very guts of the business itself to make a meaningful and enduring difference."

Besides not being the only prime movers of our organizations, very little of what we know as leaders can be said to be really our own. Our language, culture, education, and beliefs have all come to us through others. We have acquired them through relationships. Those who say they are truly "self-made leaders" are ignoring many generations of people before them.

BALANCING PERSONAL POWER WITH SYNERGY POWER AND CONTRIBUTION POWER

One of the crucial development challenges for most leaders is learning how to authentically self-express in a manner that creates value. This is not to say that leaders are not getting results—they usually are. What is missing are results that are adding value and contribution at the same time. How often do leaders get results but leave a wake of bodies in the process? How often do businesses get results and leave people or the environment damaged? This is getting results without creating value, without making a contribution. This is getting results in the absence of serving the interests of many relationships or constituencies.

INSIGHTS • REFLECTIONS • COMMITMENTS •

Leaders need to make this crucial development shift by balancing their personal power (authentic self-expression) with synergy power and contribution power (creating value). If leaders attempt to use their personal power to achieve results while ignoring synergy power—a common dominant, driven leadership style—real contribution and a people-centered culture are sacrificed on the altar of immediate achievement.

Most organizations today take a very mechanistic approach to this model. Many companies tend to focus on results at all costs and drive the organization and people to support these goals.

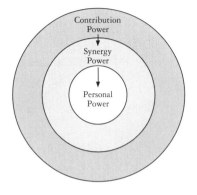

This mechanistic approach values results over synergy and synergy over the individual. It's an outside-in view of organizations and people. This approach to leading organizations results in people feeling devalued and wondering, "Where do I fit in? Why am I here?" It's an approach to leadership that misses the power of human capital.

An organic approach to business sees people as the source of creativity and dynamism. In this type of organization, personal power supports synergy

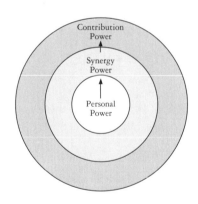

power, which in turn creates value-added contribution to customers, employees, and the environment. This inside-out model of organizations creates a purposeful culture where people are constantly thinking, "How can I make more of a contribution? How can I apply my gifts with others to make a difference?" It's a purposeful, dynamic approach to organizational leadership that values and leverages the power of human capital.

Unfortunately, many leaders are limiting their effectiveness by using only their personal power to drive for results. In the process they have adopted a tough, get-it-done persona—devoid of much emotional intelligence. Winning at all costs rules the day, and relationships are seen as a means to an end—getting the results. Unknowingly, sustainable results are being compromised on a long-term basis because the synergy power of the organization declines.

I recently spoke to a CEO who had started to build his bridge from personal power to synergy power. After a long struggle "to set his organization right," he finally had to change his approach and value the power of synergy. Describing his experience, he told me, "My rules just weren't working anymore. The more I tried to assert my will, the worse things got. Not only was I attempting to take total responsibility for the turnaround, I also was taking the total blame for any problems. I was amazingly self-centered. I believed the fate of the entire business was mine alone. Letting go of that belief freed me to really lead us to a new future." Peter Block, in his book *Stewardship,* wrote, "We are reluctant to let go of the belief that 'if I am to care for something, I must control it.'"

Paul Walsh, Chairman and CEO of Pillsbury, described it to me this way: "As managers, we are trained as cops who are supposed to keep things under control. As leaders, we need to shift from control to trust." Giving an apt description of balancing personal power with synergy power, he went on to say, "I don't care who you are or how great you are—no one person can totally claim the victory or totally abstain from the defeat."

INSIGHTS • REFLECTIONS • COMMITMENTS •

Learning to move our belief from thinking "I have all the answers" to "together we have all the answers" is the first crucial step in Interpersonal Mastery.

REDUCING THE INTENTION–PERCEPTION GAP

The second step for leaders is to realize that we often lack *full awareness* of our impact on others. We assume to an amazing degree that other people clearly and fully receive our intended communication. It's a *huge* leap of faith that does not hold up under sufficient investigation. Have you ever had a great laugh with a group of people and then asked each person why they thought it was so funny? Probably you were surprised to discover the unique perspective from which each person interprets the world.

Growth, change, and ultimately evolution occur as individuals, organizations, and society increase the depth of their relationships by continually broadening and strengthening their interdependent connections.

—Beth Jarman and George Land

All of us have been communicating our intentions since we delivered our first kick in our mother's womb. Since then, our rich, well-practiced internal conversations have evolved considerably, and we take for granted that others are receiving precisely our intended meaning. We express ourselves, and then we are shocked when our messages are misunderstood. Emerson wrote: "Men imagine that they communicate their virtue or vice only by overt actions, and do not see that virtue or vice emit a breath every moment."

Becoming skilled at receiving feedback from others becomes crucial to ensure that our self-expression is adding value. Effective leadership requires us to constantly reduce the gap between intended and perceived communication. As one CEO likes to remind me, "I always start with API—Assumption of Positive Intent. Ninety-nine point nine percent of the leaders I know want to do well for themselves and others." Although most leaders have good intentions, how these intentions are received can be quite different above, below, and across from them in the organization.

BEYOND 360° FEEDBACK TO 720° DEGREE FEEDBACK

The tool most organizations use to help leaders deal with the intention-perception gap is 360° feedback. With such programs, leaders are given feedback from multiple sources on their behavior, skills, and leadership approaches.

Unfortunately, 360° feedback does not reveal the full horizon. From a development perspective, it only reveals a portion of the person, rather than a total picture. This is particularly true when it is the sole source of self-understanding given to the leader. If a development process is modeled primarily around 360° feedback, executives only learn how to create themselves in the image of others. As a result, they learn how to *act* instead of how to *be*—a direct route to following versus leading. In a provocative way, I tell most of my client organizations, "You don't need 360° feedback. What you need for your leaders is *720° Feedback*." After they give me a polite, somewhat confused stare, I elaborate that 360° feedback in the absence of new self-knowledge often has two limitations:

1. It can create a defensive reaction, and therefore no growth takes place.
2. It encourages people to simply deliver the desired behaviors without giving them the personal insight to grow—a formula destined to limit authentic self-expression by creating actors versus leaders.

INSIGHTS • REFLECTIONS • COMMITMENTS •

But *720° Feedback* is different. It begins with an *Inner 360°*—a deep, broad, well-integrated understanding of ourselves, as well as our current and desired stages of development. This first stage ensures that we begin to master a more authentic understanding of ourselves. Then, an *Outer 360°* is completed to give broad feedback on how people above, across, and below us perceive our strengths and areas of development. With *720° Feedback*, leaders now have a context to interpret the input of others.

For instance, I worked with a vice president of a consumer products company, who prior to our coaching received 360° feedback from his company. He was perceived as too aggressive and not trustworthy. He was devastated by the feedback because he lacked the self-knowledge to meaningfully interpret the harsh input. He had no idea what to do.

Should he pull back on his relationships (be less aggressive)? If he did that, wouldn't it further erode his sense of trust with people? Since he didn't know himself at a deep enough level, he was unable to assimilate the feedback, and he was totally paralyzed developmentally.

We're all in this together, by ourselves!

—Lily Tomlin

After completing our *Executive to Leader Institute* and getting an integrated 720-degree view of himself, his entire situation clarified. For the first time, he became objectively aware that he was extremely aggressive and dominant. He had no idea his interpersonal style was so far beyond the norm for leaders. Suddenly he had a context to understand the value of this part of the feedback, and he was motivated to show up in a manner more consistent with his real intentions. Regarding the trustworthiness factor, we found in the *Inner 360°* that he was a very honest person of high integrity. However, his somewhat introverted, aloof approach with people was creating a perception that he held things back. Knowing this, the challenge was of a different order. He needed to spend more time with relationships across from him to let people get to know him. Once he got the complete *720° Feedback*, he was able to engage actively in a development plan to move forward.

INTIMATE CONNECTION OF PERSONAL MASTERY AND INTERPERSONAL MASTERY

The best way to solicit feedback from others is not to wait for a "big event" like a 360° feedback program—do it in real time. As you are expressing yourself, you are adding value by watching for cues of discomfort, misunderstanding, or inappropriate silence from people. Ask them for their feedback on your views and how you are coming across. Even if you are quite sure people are listening, ask them what they think. Encourage people to challenge you. Ask people if there are other ways to view this. Don't assume. Make sure they have received your intentions. If not, ask them what they heard, and then take the time to clarify until you are satisfied your intentions have been received. This will serve a three fold purpose:

1. Your self-expression will be even more authentic and create more value.
2. You will learn more about how you are being perceived.
3. You will develop more effective ways to communicate.

Herodotus summed up the intention-perception gap well when he wrote, "When men dream, each has his own world. When they are awake, they have a common world." Commit to waking up, and also commit to ensuring that others are awake with you.

BUILDING AWARENESS OF HOW YOU INTERPRET AND PROCESS YOUR WORLD

As you can see, Personal Mastery and Interpersonal Mastery are intimately connected. As we grow as people, we grow in relationship. As we grow in relationship, we grow as people. The intervening dynamic between ourselves and others is our structure of interpretation—our unique set of beliefs, fears, and personal constructs through which we process or filter our world. We rarely see the world as it is; we principally see the world through the lens of who we are. As a result, if we want to become more effective in relationships, we need to become more aware of how we are interpreting these interactions. One of the most helpful ways to build this awareness is to reflect on two fundamental questions as you relate to people:

- How is my behavior opening up possibilities?
- How is my behavior shutting down possibilities?

INSIGHTS • REFLECTIONS • COMMITMENTS •

Assuming the person you are relating to has positive or neutral intentions, if your behavior opens up possibilities then you are probably In-Character and your inter-action will lead to openness, compassion, inclusion, and win-win outcomes. If, on the other hand, your behavior is shutting down possibilities, you are probably In-Persona and your relationships will be guided by image, control, anger, conflict, restriction, and self-interest. You may remember that persona protects. In its effort to "protect us," it also can separate us from others. It can create a wall, a distance between us and those around us. Committing ourselves to more open-ness, making our persona more permeable, is the doorway to Interpersonal Mastery.

> *Treat people as if they were what they ought to be, and you help them to become what they are capable of being.*
>
> —Goethe

I was driving along a parkway around a lake in Minneapolis on a brilliant spring day. As you may know, spring in Minneapolis is quite dramatic and transformative. From the depths of winter, everything explodes into life. Seemingly all at once, the trees bloom and the birds return. As I was driving along enjoying all of this, a big fat robin flew into the front grille of my car and was killed immediately. I pulled over to check it out, and there was nothing I could do. As I drove away, I started to think that just a moment ago this beautiful bird had been singing her joyous song with all her being, enjoying her life, tending to her family, expressing her purpose. In a flash, I came along and unintentionally shut all of that down. How often do we do that in our relationships? How often as leaders do we come barreling through our organi-zations and kill the songs people have to sing? If we are honest, we will admit that we all do it more often than we care to imagine.

How do we go about encouraging all the "songs to be sung" around us? The most crucial quality of character in a leader is openness—openness to new possibilities in the marketplace, openness to new approaches and strategies, openness to relation-ships, openness to new ways of doing things, openness to letting people express their "songs." It's so important to leadership, maybe we should stop calling people "leaders" and rename them "openers." Leaders open up or shut down opportunities in direct proportion to how open or shut down they are to themselves.

We worked with a senior executive a while ago who sincerely believed in openness. What he didn't realize was that his way of being direct and frank with people was actually shutting them down. He believed in openness and authenticity, but his approach was creating the opposite effect. It was a total mystery to him. He even rationalized it by saying that *other people* in his organization just weren't as open as he was. What was missing was openness to himself. He could be open and direct when it came to driving people to results. He could not be open about his fears, limitations, inadequacies, or unexpressed possibilities. As a result, his "openness" was very limited. Once he gained the inner strength and confidence to be more vulnerable and open about his real concerns and feelings in situations, it came as a great surprise to him how other people then opened up to him. He shared with me, "It was startling to me that people opened up and supported me as I opened up and shared my vulnerabilities. I built my career by being invulnerable. I was very open about the work, but very fearful about revealing myself. But I didn't understand that I was distancing people in the process. I now understand that more openness in the organization begins with me."

INSIGHTS • REFLECTIONS • COMMITMENTS •

Anne Morrow Lindbergh wrote, "When one is a stranger to oneself, then one is estranged from others, too. If one is out of touch with oneself, then one cannot touch others." As an international consultant, Sara really touched her clients. When asked why her clients had such outstanding regard for her, she quickly replied, "I treat each one with the respect of an honored guest. I feel privileged to be associated with them and want them to feel served. I can't fully explain it; I just treat them like a guest in my home." Unfortunately, Sara's co-workers reported that they did not feel like guests. They felt that Sara only cared about "looking special" in her clients' eyes and cared very little about them. Sara was not aware of her excessive need to "be special." This need was generated by her Shadow Belief "I'm not good enough as I am."

Want to lead with purpose?
Serve with your whole heart.

—Joe Eastman

As a result, Sara was driven to validate her specialness from the outside. Once she understood this dynamic and comprehended emotionally how mistreated her co-workers felt, she was very motivated to treat everyone in her life as "guests." She worked on her limiting beliefs and changed her relationship paradigm from one of self-service to one of other-service.

The goal of Interpersonal Mastery is to shift our focus from self-fulfillment to one of service-fulfillment. It is centered in purpose—how we can serve others to make a difference in the world. Commenting on our excessive focus on personal fulfillment to the exclusion of everything else, Daniel Yankelovich wrote:

> Many people today are striving to expand their lives by reaching beyond the self, but they are doing so with an ever-narrowing attitude of egocentrism that eventually constricts them. People unwittingly bring a set of flawed psychological premises to the quest for self-fulfillment—in particular, the premise that the human self is a hierarchy of inner needs, and self-fulfillment is an inner journey to discover them. This premise is rarely questioned or examined, even though it frequently leads people to defeat their goal and become isolated and anxious instead of fulfilled. Looking beyond one's personal search for meaning in life in terms of maintaining meaningful relationships with others is an important part of the growth process."

Increase your awareness of how to develop and to build relationships more effectively as a leader by taking some time to reflect on the following exercises.

REFLECTION

INTERPERSONAL MASTERY

Opening Up or Shutting Down Communication

1. Under what conditions do you shut down communication?

2. What beliefs are causing you to shut down?

3. How can you be more open in future situations?

4. Under what conditions do you inhibit your own self-expression?

5. What personal beliefs are causing you to hold back?

6. How can you be more expressive in future situations?

7. How effectively are your relationships building a bridge to connect your authentic self-expression with your desire to create value?

8. How can you more effectively build your relationship bridges?

THE FIVE TOUCHSTONES OF AUTHENTIC LEADERSHIP

A few years ago, I was reflecting on the value of relationships for leaders and thinking, "What is the central core of effective relationships?" After analyzing it every which way, it hit me with profound simplicity: *Authenticity* is the key. Can you imagine a healthy, functioning relationship or a healthy, functioning team that lacks authenticity? Authenticity is the core of relationships around which

> *Leaders must attend to one key growth question: How authentically am I showing up in the world and in my organization?*
>
> —Tom Gegax

synergy and trust grow. Imagine a relationship without authenticity. Can it survive? Certainly not long term. Authenticity is the life force of relationships. Authenticity is the true voice of the leader as it touches other people's hearts. From observing authentic leaders, I would suggest there are *Five Touchstones of Authentic Leadership* which are crucial to building the interpersonal bridge from authentic self-expression to creating value:

1. Touchstone One: Know Yourself Authentically: Throughout the ages the phrase *nosce teipsum*, know thyself, appears over and over in the writings of Ovid, Cicero, and Socrates, in the sayings of the Seven Sages of Greece, on the entrance to the temple of Apollo, in Christian writings, and in Eastern texts. One scholar says it was part of Shakespeare's "regular moral and religious diet."

Nosce teipsum threads its way through history as the pre-eminent precept in life. Chaucer: "Full wise is he that can himself know." Browning: "Trust is within ourselves." Pope: "And all our knowledge is, ourselves to know." Montaigne: "If a man does not know himself, how should he know his functions and his powers?" de Saint-Exupéry: "Each man must look to himself to teach him the meaning of life." Lao Tzu: "Knowledge of self is the source of our abilities."

Contemporary thinkers from Ralph Waldo Emerson to Abraham Maslow to Warren Bennis to Stephen R. Covey have all carried on the tradition. Emerson wrote, "The purpose of life seems to be to acquaint man with himself." Bennis writes: "Letting the self emerge is the essential task of leaders." Covey says, "It is futile to put personality ahead of character, to try to improve relationships with others before improving ourselves."

If we want to be more effective with others, we first need to become more effective with ourselves. Instead of focusing on finding the right partner (in business or friendships) seek to *be* the right partner. Commit to getting to know your total self authentically through Personal Mastery. Practice being what you wish others to become.

2. Touchstone Two: Listen Authentically: How often are we truly present with someone? How often do we set aside all our concerns—past, present, and future—

and completely "be there" for someone else? How often do we *really hear* what the other person is saying and feeling versus filtering it heavily through our own immediate concerns and time pressures? Authentic listening is not easy. We hear the words, but rarely do we really listen. We hear the words, but do we also "hear" the emotions, fears, underlying concerns? Authentic listening is not a technique. It is centered in compassion and in a concern for the other person which goes beyond our self-centered needs. Listening authentically is centered in the principle of psychological reciprocity: to influence others, we must first be open to their influence. Authentic listening is the attempt, as Stephen R. Covey puts it, "To understand first and be understood second." It places the *other person's* self-expression as primary at that moment. Authentic listening is about being generous—listening with a giving attitude that seeks to bring forth the contribution in someone versus listening with our limiting assessments, opinions, and judgments. Authentic listening is about being open to the purpose and learning coming to us through the other person.

INSIGHTS • REFLECTIONS • COMMITMENTS •

I find it amusing to observe leaders who think that not speaking is the same as really listening. Fidgeting in their chairs and doing several things at once, many leaders give numerous, simultaneous cues that they are anywhere but present with people. One successful senior executive I was about to coach on how others perceived his poor listening skills was so agitated while listening to me, he actually threw his pen across the room. His impatience and inner distress were so strong, he couldn't even listen to me for a minute without his "disease" bursting through his body and making him fling his Montblanc across my

Effective leaders put words to the formless longings and deeply felt needs of others.

—Warren Bennis

office! It was a very embarrassing moment for him to see precisely what other people saw in his behavior. Over time, he learned to relax more and set aside his internal dialogue and time pressure to be more present with people.

Try practicing authentic listening. Be with people and have the goal to fully understand the thoughts and feelings they are trying to express. Use your comments to draw them out, to open them up, and to clarify what is said versus expressing your view, closing them down, and saying only what you want. Not only will this help you to understand what value and contribution the other person has, it will create a new openness in the relationship which will allow you to self-express more authentically, as well.

Authentic listening creates the platform for true synergy and team effectiveness. Being open to valuing and attending to different perspectives from diverse sources results in a more complete understanding of issues and more effective decisions. Authentic listening is the soul of synergy.

3. Touchstone Three: Express Authentically: Authentic expression is a delicate subject for many leaders. I have yet to meet a leader who would admit readily that he or she lacks some degree of integrity. I also have yet to meet a leader who has complete integrity in all parts of his or her life. Integrity goes far beyond telling the truth. Integrity means total congruence between who we are and what we do. It is a formidable goal, and most of us will spend our lifetime on the path to getting there. How often have we held back something that we feel is important because we are fearful of expressing it? How often have we expressed something in a slightly more favorable light? How often have we protected someone from what we consider a tough message? How often have we feigned modesty for something we were really proud of?

Authentic expression is the true voice of the leader. We speak it from our character, and it creates trust, synergy, and connection with everyone around us. Authentic expression is *not* about refining our presentation style—it's deeper than that. Some of the most authentic leaders I know stumble around a bit in their delivery, but the words come right from their hearts and experiences. You can feel it. You feel their conviction and the integral connection of who they are and what they say. Benjamin Franklin wrote, "Think innocently and justly, and, if you speak, speak accordingly."

INSIGHTS • REFLECTIONS • COMMITMENTS •

Expressing authentically is about straight talk that creates value. It's not about hurting people with bluntness or insensitivity. Expressing authentically is sharing your real thoughts and feelings in a manner which opens up possibilities. It's not about delivering only positive messages and avoiding the negatives—sometimes the most difficult messages can open up the most possibilities if shared in a thoughtful, compassionate manner. Expressing authentically is what Gus Blanchard, CEO of Deluxe Corporation, calls "caring confrontation"—the unique blending of straight talk with a genuine concern for people. Like many leaders, Blanchard had been uncomfortable with such interaction for years. As his career progressed, he realized, "Real caring involves giving people the tough feedback they need to grow." Al Schuman, President and CEO of Ecolab, supports this view: "A leader's ability to be appropriately tough is directly proportional to the depth and quality of his or her relationships." Carl Jung said it this way: "To confront a person in his shadow is to show him his light."

> *A truly effective leader creates an environment that sustains the mission of the organization while increasing the happiness quotient of shareholders, employees, customers, suppliers, and the community.*
>
> —Bob Kidder

Start observing how authentically you are expressing yourself. How are you doing with your requests and with your promises? Fernando Flores, communication expert and President of Business Design Associates, boiled down his communication paradigm to this: "A human society operates through the expression of requests and promises." Are you authentically expressing your requests? Are you authentically fulfilling your promises? Use this model as a guide to authentic self-expression; it is very powerful.

In other areas of expressing yourself authentically, are you adding a positive spin here or withholding something there? How can you effectively deliver a tough message to someone with warmth and concern? Are you willing to risk revealing your fears and vulnerabilities to express how you are really feeling? If you commit to expressing authenticity, you will not come away from relationships the same as you went in—you will come away having opened up possibilities and having created new value.

4. Touchstone Four: Appreciate Authentically: As leaders, we do too much and appreciate too little. Has anyone ever appreciated you too much? It would probably be safe to say that human beings have an infinite capacity to be appreciated. Lenny Bruce wrote, "There are never enough 'I love you's.' " A mentor of mine once told me, "Love is an extreme case of appreciation." However, as leaders we don't appreciate enough, much less love enough. In fact, we have banned the "L" word from business. In spite of the fact that the "L" word is the substance that unifies teams, builds cultures, fosters commitment, and bonds people to an organization, it is not socially acceptable even to say the "L" word in a business context. We can say we hate someone with no repercussions, but if we say we love someone, we may be banished for life! In lieu of this cultural taboo, let's use the word "appreciation." Appreciation is one type of self-expression that creates value. It energizes people and makes people want to exceed their goals and perceived limits. Criticism is one type of self-expression that usually does not add value. What it does add is fear and insecurity. Criticism may get short-term results, but it does not add long-term

value. Judging others critically doesn't define them anyway, it defines ourselves. As the Islamic saying goes, "A thankful person is thankful under all circumstances. A complaining soul complains even if he lives in paradise."

As leaders, we need to follow the advice of William Penn, "If there is any kindness I can show, or any good thing I can do to any fellow being, let me do it now, and not deter or neglect it, as I shall not pass this way again." What would an organization or team be like if people willingly expressed this type of appreciation for one another?

Studies done by John Gottmann and described in his book, *Why Marriages Succeed and Why Marriages Fail*, found that relationships which had a 5 to 1 ratio of appreciation to criticism were thriving, healthy, and productive. However, relationships that were at a 1 to 1 ratio of appreciation to criticism were doomed to failure. Divorces were the inevitable result of falling to a 1 to 1 ratio or lower.

INSIGHTS • REFLECTIONS • COMMITMENTS •

Practice appreciating authentically. Look for what is going well—point it out and have some fun celebrating the good things as they come up. Shift your analysis of situations from finding fault to finding the value being added. Acknowledge effort and intention even if the results are occasionally lacking. Trust that your appreciation will energize people. Commit to a culture of acknowledgment and appreciation—have team members commit to being a source of acknowledgment and appreciation to one another. Learn to give, receive, and encourage appreciation.

> *One need ask only one question, "What for? What am I to unify my being for?" The reply is: Not for my own sake.*
>
> —Martin Buber

5. Touchstone Five: Serve Authentically: As David Prosser, Chairman of RTW, shared with me, "I think one of the key questions every leader must ask himself or herself is, 'How do I want to be of service to others?'"

Ultimately, a leader is not judged so much by how well he or she leads, but by how well he or she serves. All value and contribution are achieved through service. Do we have any other purpose in life but to serve? As leaders, we may think we're "leading," but in reality we're serving. Leadership is a continuum of service. We serve our organization. We serve our people. We serve our customers. We serve our marketplace. We serve our community. We serve our family. We serve our relationships. At the heart of service is the principle of interdependence: Relationships are effective when mutual benefits are served.

Capturing the essence of serving authentically, Peter Block writes in *Stewardship*, "There is pride in leadership, it evokes images of direction. There is humility in stewardship, it evokes images of service. Service is central to the idea of stewardship."

As leaders, when we move from control to service, we acknowledge that we are not the central origin of achievement. This shift is an emotional and spiritual breakthrough. Life flows through us, and we simply play our role. Our real job is to serve all the constituencies in our life and, in the process, to appreciate genuinely the fact that only through our interdependence with others do we create value. The more we serve and appreciate others, the more we coopera-tively generate value-added contribution.

As leaders, if we live for ourselves, we will only have ourselves for support. If we live for our organization, we will have people for support. If we live for the world, the whole universe will support us. Serve with purpose and you will marshal far-reaching resources.

A friend of mine had been seeking an oppor-tunity to teach her son about the value of ser-vice and giving. The opportunity presented itself after the young boy's birthday party as he prepared to devour one of his gifts: a multi-layered box of chocolates. Approaching her son, my friend asked, "Are you happy with this gift?" Wild-eyed, he immediately responded, "Oh, yes!" My friend probed, "What would make you even happier?" Her son had no idea what possibly could add to his joy. His mother then said, "If you gave some-one else a chocolate, they would be as happy as you are, and you could feel even happier." The young boy thought for a minute and said, "Let's go see grandma at the nursing home." Off they went to the nursing home. When the child saw the joy on his grandmother's face and felt how it multiplied his joy, he was hooked. Before he left the nursing home, the entire box was gone, and the boy had learned the power and joy of service.

INSIGHTS • REFLECTIONS • COMMITMENTS •

Practice serving authentically. Start by appreciating that there are forces beyond you guiding the whole process. Understand that you are fortunate to have this particular role. Appreciate it; then let your talents and gifts come forth. Bryant Hinckley summed it up well in *Hours with Our Leaders:*

Life's most urgent question is, "What are you doing for others?"

—Martin Luther King, Jr.

Service is the virtue that distinguished the great of all times and which they will be remembered by. It places a mark of nobility upon its disciples. It is the dividing line which separates the two great groups of the world—those who help and those who hinder, those who lift and those who lean, those who contribute and those who only consume. How much better it is to give than to receive. Service in any form is comely and beautiful. To give encouragement, to impart sympathy, to show interest, to banish fear, to build self-confidence and awaken hope in the hearts of others, in short—to love them and to show it—is to render the most precious service.

LEADERSHIP GROWTH COMMITMENTS

INTERPERSONAL MASTERY

Reflect on the learnings that have surfaced as you read this chapter. Identify three leadership growth commitments to enhance your relationships. Then identify the potential obstacles, resources needed, and signs or measures of success.

1. Key Learnings:
   A. _____
   B. _____
   C. _____

2. Leadership Growth Commitments:
   A. _____
   B. _____
   C. _____

3. Resources Needed:
   A. _____
   B. _____
   C. _____

4. Potential Obstacles:
   A. _____
   B. _____
   C. _____

5. Timeline and Measures of Success:
   A. _____
   B. _____
   C. _____

Interpersonal Mastery
Summary

- *Build Relationship Bridges:* Relationships are the bridges between authentic self-expression and creating value. Leaders lead by virtue of who they are, but create value by virtue of their relationships.

- *Balance Personal Power with Synergy Power and Contribution Power:* Using your personal power to get results is not enough. Balancing your personal power with synergy power to make a life-enriching contribution is the key to authentic leadership.

- *Build Awareness of Intention-Perception Gap:* We often are not fully aware of our total impact on others. Commit yourself to *720° Feedback* to grow as a leader.

- *Personal Mastery and Interpersonal Mastery are Intimately Connected:* As we grow as a person, our relationships grow. As our relationships grow, we grow as a person. As both grow, we lead more effectively.

- *Become Aware of Your Structure of Interpretation:* Commit yourself to the endless discovery of how you process your world. We lead and relate based on how we interpret our life experiences through the lens of our personal beliefs.

- *Practice the Five Touchstones to Authentic Leadership:* Know yourself authentically, listen authentically, express authentically, appreciate authentically, serve authentically.

Pathway Five: Being Mastery

Leading Through Being

*Being Mastery is connecting with the silence and peace of
the innermost depth of one's character to support more
dynamism, effectiveness, and contribution.*

Being is our true nature, our core, our source, our inner Self. Being is the
essence at the deepest level of our character supporting all action and achievement. Understanding and unfolding our inner Self—our Being—may be unfamiliar territory to many people. However, practices for gaining familiarity
with Being can be learned.

Personal Journey into Being

Exploring Being is an ongoing journey that is particularly helpful to leading
from within. Early in my life, I learned to explore my Being through meditation. Although meditation is a technique that works for me, it certainly is not
the only one. Many other ways are just as effective and easily accessible to us in
our everyday lives. We will consider some of these later on in this chapter.
Regardless of the technique or techniques we choose, it's important to understand that these practices are merely bridges to Being Mastery.

For several months in 1972, I lived in a small room on the Atlantic coast of
Spain. However, that's only the superficial description of what I was doing
there. What I was really doing was non-doing. I was learning to go into the
silence of Being.

Looking back, it was one of the most intense, valuable times of my life.
Although I didn't comprehend it fully then, I was fostering an inner silence that
would last a lifetime. I was learning to live in the eye of the hurricane of life.

Day after day, week after week, month after month, I explored the depths of consciousness. This journey took me so deeply into the silence and stillness of my inner Self, after the third week my pulse dropped to thirty-two beats per minute while my eyes were open! The combination of inner wakefulness and physical rest transformed me. For the first time in my life, I comprehended that life evolves from the inside out. I was aware of how my fears and anxieties were created within. I experienced inner blocks, and I learned to free myself from them to permit energy to flow naturally. I discovered a new type of happiness which was unattached to any external event or object. Stress, fatigue, and tension were dissolved by the profound restfulness of going within. It became clear to me how life is created within and projected outside.

> *Within you there is a stillness and sanctuary to which you can retreat at anytime and be yourself.*
>
> —The Dhammapada

During this meditation course our group spent each evening with Maharishi Mahesh Yogi. He encouraged us to share our experiences and to ask questions. Spending my days immersed in the depth of my inner Self was a wonderful experience. Spending the evenings with such a wise teacher was pure magic. The sessions were free flowing. We covered everything from the purpose of life to higher states of consciousness to the meaning of spirituality. I particularly remember one evening when Maharishi was guiding us through how the inner life supported the outer, and he said, "The son of a millionaire is not born to be poor. Man is born to enjoy. He's born of Bliss, of Consciousness, of Wisdom, of Creativity. It's a matter of choice whether we shiver in the cold on the verandah or are happy in the warmth of the living room. As long as the outer life is connected with the inner values of Being, then all the avenues of outer life will be rich and glorious." Insight and wisdom like this filled those evenings during which I received more practical knowledge crucial to my success than I learned throughout my academic career.

TAMING THE THOUGHT MONKEYS

Writing about inner Being is no small task. Trying to describe something at the basis of all our experience is a very round, slippery "thing." As I sat down to try for the first time, my mind was so full of thoughts about what to write, it was jumping in every direction at once. I wasn't suffering from writer's block. It was something just as unproductive; lack of focus combined with lack of broad comprehension. My mind was like a bunch of mischievous monkeys jumping from one tree to another but never finding the fruit to satisfy them. At first, I tried to discipline myself and to focus my attention, but this effort was to no avail—the "monkeys" continued to chase one another. I knew better than to try to chase them out—they love to play that game and only get more excited. I decided instead to give the "creatures of thought" the fruit they were looking for. I sat down to meditate. As I settled into deeper, more silent and powerful levels of thought, the jungle of my mind transformed. The "thought monkeys" naturally settled down as they enjoyed the nourishment of profound levels of thought. In this less-bound state of awareness, I comprehended the entire chapter and organized it effortlessly. In this more expanded state, everything was easily sorted out—all the divergent ideas connected. Each seemingly unrelated thought came into context in this quiet, settled state of awareness. By going into my inner Self, my Being, I allowed clarity and comprehension to surface naturally, and I no longer struggled to control the process.

INSIGHTS • REFLECTIONS • COMMITMENTS •

GOING TO ANOTHER LEVEL TO RESOLVE LEADERSHIP CHALLENGES

Connecting with our inner Being to comprehend all sorts of life situations is so natural a process, we may not even be aware of it. Have you ever had the experience of losing your car keys and running around the house, frantically checking over and over all the common places you put them? Exasperated, you give up, sit down, and close your eyes to compose yourself. In this easy, free state of mind, the obscure location of the keys appears. Similarly, have you ever anguished over a very complex problem and while you're out for a walk in a relaxed state the solution rolls out at your feet? As we go within, the power of thought is greater. Just as atomic levels are more powerful than molecular levels, our deeper levels of thought have more energy and power. It's the third law of thermodynamics: As activity decreases, order increases. As the mind settles down it becomes more orderly, more able to comprehend and to handle difficult challenges.

All man's miseries derive from not being able to sit quietly in a room alone.

—Blaise Pascal

GETTING THINGS DONE BY NON-DOING

The toughest problems we face are rarely solved on their own level. The mind needs to go to a more profound, more comprehensive level to get "above and around them." It never ceases to amaze me how much "work" can get done by "non-work." For most leaders, the best ideas and great solutions usually don't arise during traditional work hours, but during the quiet, inner moments while swimming, running, walking, or meditating. The mind is loose, settled, relaxed, and able to comprehend the parts and the whole at the same time. The president of a consumer products firm related to me how his daily swims were "Zen-like experiences where I peacefully sort out very difficult and complex issues. I don't even go to the pool to 'do' anything. It just happens when I get into that calm, yet aware state." As Wolfgang Amadeus Mozart wrote, "When I am, as it were, completely myself, entirely alone, and of good cheer—say traveling in a carriage or walking after a good meal . . . it is on such occasions that ideas flow best and most abundantly."

THE SEARCH FOR SOMETHING MORE

As leaders, how often do we take the time to relax and to think? Our job is to be above and beyond the daily grind, but often we are immersed in only the doing. Can leaders expect to be ahead of the strategic curve when we rarely get a chance to catch our breath and think in new ways? A while ago, I was talking to Paul Walsh, Chairman and CEO of Pillsbury, about what he thought leaders in the next millennium would require. He quickly responded, "More time to reflect and to think provocatively about current and future dynamics." Another CEO put it this way, "As leaders, our real challenge is to carve out more time to think and more time to be. When we do it, we're more refreshed and more creative. Unfortunately, we get caught up in achieving and sometimes forget where our energy and creativity come from." Leaders are constantly searching for something more. We want more achievement, more happiness, more fulfillment.

INSIGHTS • REFLECTIONS • COMMITMENTS •

It is a natural tendency. The crucial thing, however, is how we satisfy this inherent desire for more. Do we attempt to "fill ourselves up" from the outside in? Or are we able to give ourselves something really satisfying from the inside out?

Mastery of Being is that "something more" we can "give" ourselves in a self-sufficient way. It is about learning to transform our state of awareness to greater happiness and satisfaction by ourselves. No outside intervention or stimulation is required. We can do it all *by ourselves* with no harmful side effects. Imagine having the power to transform yourself physically and emotionally when you are feeling tired and stressed. That's the power of Being. Imagine problems turning to opportunities, irritation to compassion, alienation to connection. So, why don't we connect more with this state of Being?

DON'T PLACE "DESCARTES" BEFORE "THE SOURCE"

Our fast-moving, never-catch-your-breath, externally focused culture is designed "perfectly" to avoid genuine contact with the deeper levels of ourselves. The background and foreground "noise" of our lives is so dominant, we rarely get a chance to connect with any silence within us. In fact, we have become so stimulation-oriented that even our "fun" and "happiness" have become associated with ever-increasing high doses of artificial distraction. Most people go on vacations having so much *fun* that they return exhausted! Others strap large rubber bands to themselves and then jump off bridges to experience "the thrill of living"! Although fun, work, achievement, play, and exhilaration are all important parts of a fulfilling life, too often these experiences are an addictive search for the next stimulating experience to fill the void inside. We become "junkies" to external stimulation—always seeking our next "fix" to make us feel good. This type of "I'm stimulated; therefore I am" mentality often lacks the true joy of living. We have become a world of *human doers* having lost connection to our heritage as *human beings*.

> *No amount of human having or human doing can make up for a deficit in human being.*
>
> —John Adams

Many people probably would agree with Descartes: "I think, therefore I am." But Being Mastery has a different view: "I am, therefore I think." To be alive, to be effective, to be fulfilled, first requires a state of Being. Therefore, Being Mastery does not place Descartes before the Source.

Thinking is the effect; Being is the cause. Being is consciousness in its pure form, the source of thought. It is not a thought; it is the source of thought. It is not an experience; it is experience itself. In *No Man Is an Island*, Thomas Merton wrote:

> We are warmed by fire, not by the smoke of the fire. We are carried over the sea by ship, not by the wake of a ship. So too, what we are is sought in the depths of our own Being, not in our outward reflection of our own acts. We must find our real selves not in the froth stirred up by the impact of our Being upon the beings or things around us, but in our own Being which is the principle of all our acts.
>
> I do not need to see myself, I merely need to be myself. I must think and act like a living Being, but I must not plunge my whole self into what I think and do.

People who project themselves entirely into activity, and seek themselves entirely outside themselves, are like madmen who sleep on the sidewalk in front of their houses instead of living inside where it is quiet and warm.

Techniques to Unfold Being

Being is the transformational journey from here to here. Since Being is universally present, we really don't *go* anywhere. We open our awareness to our true potentiality. Being is the awareness of the eternally present moment at the basis of our experience. It is the movie screen on which our life is projected. As a Zen poem describes it:

INSIGHTS • REFLECTIONS • COMMITMENTS •

> Before my journey—mountains were
> mountains and trees were trees.
> While on my journey—mountains were no
> longer just mountains and trees no longer just trees.
> When my journey was over—mountains were
> once more mountains and trees once more trees!

To understand the practical relationship of Being in our lives, we need to look at our everyday experience. Most of us would agree that successful action is based on effective thinking. If our thoughts are clear and focused, then our actions will be precise and effective. But on the days we do not feel well, our thoughts are less effective and our actions less successful. So *feeling* is more fundamental than *thinking*; feeling gives rise to thinking, which gives rise to action. Feeling, thinking, and action all have one thing in common—they always are changing. Sometimes we feel great, think clearly, and act effectively. Other times, we do not. But feeling, thinking, and action all have one non-changing "thing" in common—

Being. To feel, to think, to act, we first must Be. The pure state of Being underlies all areas of life. The more we awaken our true nature—Being—the more effective our feeling, thinking, and action. It is the foundation, the platform for a more masterful life.

Another practical way to understand the value of Being is in terms of the different states of consciousness. Typically we experience three states of consciousness: waking, dreaming, and deep sleep. Each state of consciousness has a unique state of measurable physiology. If we're awake, the body has a measurable range of physiological functioning. The same goes for dreaming and deep sleep. Being is a distinctly different state of consciousness—a fourth major state. It's a state of restful alertness where the mind is fully awake in its own nature and the body is deeply rested, even more profoundly than during deep sleep. As we stretch the mind and body to experience broader ranges of their potentialities, we eventually acquire the natural experience of Being or Pure Consciousness permeating the other three states of consciousness. As a result, we truly begin to live life from the inside out. Every experience we have is in the context of our awakened inner nature.

> *To be ourselves fully, spontaneously, and authentically, means simply to be. . . . This is far more than the colloquial meaning of the phrase "being oneself." It is the experience of Being . . . Being ourselves, we find, is being Being.*
>
> —A. H. Almaas

So how does one experience Being? There are as many paths to experience Being as there are people. Some experience it through meditation, some through prayer, others through nature, others naturally. Franz Kafka wrote:

> You need not do anything; you need not leave your room. Remain sitting at your table and listen. You don't even need to wait; just become still, quiet, and solitary, and the world will freely offer itself to you to be unmasked. It has no choice; it will roll in ecstasy at your feet.

Abraham Maslow, in *Toward a Psychology of Being*, found that self-actualized people had a high frequency of such "peak experiences." These experiences were described as: moments of great awe, pure positive happiness, when all doubts, all fears, all inhibitions, all weaknesses were left behind. They felt one with the world, pleased with it, really belonging to it, instead of being outside looking in—the feeling that they had really seen the truth, the essence of things. Maslow identified fourteen recurring themes or "values of Being" experienced by self-actualized people:

- Wholeness
- Perfection
- Completion
- Justice
- Aliveness
- Richness
- Simplicity

- Beauty
- Goodness
- Uniqueness
- Effortlessness
- Playfulness
- Truth
- Self-Sufficiency

INSIGHTS • REFLECTIONS • COMMITMENTS •

Unless these values are an everyday experience for us, we will need some assistance in gaining insights into Being. Although there are many other techniques, one of the best ways I have found is through meditation. Since meditation simply means "to think," all of us meditate. To arrive at a pure state of Being, we want to learn how to go beyond our thoughts—to transcend meditation. Meditation is a technique for helping us arrive at this state naturally.

I've practiced many forms of meditation over the years. My personal preference is the Transcendental Meditation (TM) program. It's *not* the only way to meditate, just one way that has worked well for me and many others. I was attracted to it because it was easy to learn and didn't require any belief or behavior changes. I also liked the fact that it was one of the most thoroughly researched human development programs, with more than 700 research studies documenting its benefits to mind, body, and behavior.

The practical value of meditation can best be understood in terms of its profound rest. Every night when we sleep, we leave the field of activity, close our eyes, and "transcend" our daytime activity. This settling down of mental and physical activity results in rest and stress relief which prepares us for dynamic action the next day. Profound meditation is similar with one major difference: We maintain our awareness as we experience inordinately deep rest. We experience a state of restful alertness where the mind is alert but settled, and the body is deeply rested, even more completely rested than during sleep. When we open our eyes, we feel revitalized, think more clearly, and act more effectively. When we learn to settle into our Being, we naturally become more and more ourselves. It is much like the experience of taking a refreshing bath. If the bath is truly refreshing, you are refreshed. You don't have to convince yourself you are refreshed; you do not have to create a mood of being refreshed. You don't have to believe you are refreshed. *You are refreshed*. This is *not* the power of positive thinking. It is the power of Positive Being. As William Penn wrote: "True Silence is the rest of the mind; it is to the spirit what sleep is to the body, nourishment and refreshment."

> *I think what we're seeking is an experience of being alive, so that our life experiences on the purely physical plane will have resonances within our innermost Being and reality, so that we actually feel the rapture of being alive.*
>
> —Joseph Campbell

The following reflection is *not* related to doing TM or any other formal meditation technique. It is just meant to be a small taste—an *Hors D'oeuvres* of going within. If you want the full meal, you may want to consider personal meditation instruction.

REFLECTION

BEING MASTERY

Exploring the Leader Within

Find a quiet place and sit comfortably. Close
your eyes. Stretch your body so it loosens and
relaxes. Let your awareness follow the flow of
your breathing, in and out. When your mind
wanders, gently come back to your breathing.
Observe your awareness settling down. Let your
thoughts, sensations, anxieties, and worries
appear as if on a large screen. Let your thoughts
come and go. Just return to your breathing. If
your awareness of the breathing starts to fade,
just let your awareness fade. No need to force
anything. No need to resist anything. No need
to do anything. Just be aware of the entire
process in a non-judging manner. If the "bottom drops out" and you find yourself thinking
again, you may have just transcended into
Being. Just return your awareness gently to
your breathing. After 15–20 minutes, lie down
for 5 minutes and then slowly get up. Notice
how this calm, centered, refreshed state of
awareness can permeate your activity.

CONNECTING WITH OUR INNER SELF

Several years ago, I gave a lecture entitled "Meditation and the Dynamic Life" at a university. This well-attended event attempted to present new paradigms about meditation as preparation for an effective life versus a retreat from life. The audience had so many misconceptions about meditation requiring concentration or contemplation or withdrawal from the world that the lecture went longer than expected. Since I had to speak at another event that evening and I had a long distance to travel, I cut short some of the questions, packed my car, and began my drive. Before too long, it occurred to me that if I wanted to be "at my best" for this next lecture, I needed to refresh myself. So, I pulled the car over near a dense woods. I left the car and found a soft, mossy spot, and I meditated. As my mind and body repeatedly dove into and out of deep restfulness, my freshness, clarity, and vitality returned.

> *The leader teaches more through Being than through doing. The quality of one's silence conveys more than long speeches.*
>
> —John Heider

As I was about to open my eyes and return to the car, I heard footsteps. Cracking my eyes open, I saw a large buck three to four feet away stomping his hoof and waving his head back and forth. While I was enjoying his display, a second, third, and fourth deer joined us. Before returning to the car, I enjoyed 10 to 15 minutes of observing these magnificent creatures, who didn't seem the least uncomfortable in my presence. Refreshed and renewed through my meditation, I continued my drive and arrived at my next presentation feeling revitalized. That is why connection with Being is a wonderful preparation for action. It is also a great preparation for seeing life with new eyes. As Marcel Proust wrote, "The real voyage of discovery consists not in seeing new landscapes, but in having new eyes."

Although meditation is a great way to connect with our inner potentiality, it is not the only way. Meditation is a technique to bring our mind from the surface of life to the depth of our Being. What are some other techniques? Since we're talking about a level of life that is at the basis of all our experiences, we have the potential to locate that level in any experience. So, what are the best ways to do this? I am sure you have your own paths to Being, but here are a few that work well for me:

• *Reverence for Nature*

Most of us at some time in our lives have become overwhelmed by the immensity and grandeur of nature. When we stare into the heavens on a star-filled night, gaze over the Grand Canyon, snorkel through tropical waters, or walk along a creek in our neighborhood, we experience a *moment of awe* beyond our intellectual comprehension. That moment of deep, silent, unbounded appreciation beyond and between our thoughts is the experience of inner Being. Spend time in nature and enjoy the technique of deep appreciation and wonder to stretch or extend your boundaries.

INSIGHTS • REFLECTIONS • COMMITMENTS •

• *Music*

Music, because it moves us directly and deeply, is probably the most powerful art form. It can directly open the gateway to one's soul with its organized vibrations. The vibrations that move each of us are different. Handel's Water Music or Gregorian Chants "take me away." Find the music that soothes and relaxes you the most. (I also like the Rolling Stones, but I only listen to them when I want to *express energy* rather than connect with it!) Go deeply into soothing music—it can be a wonderful way to explore your Being. T. S. Eliot wrote, "Music heard so deeply that it is not heard at all. But you are the music while the music lasts."

• *Present-Moment Awareness*

Rarely comprehending the present moment

fully, we often live our lives in the past or the future. Being is infinity contained in the eternally present moment. Thinking about Being in the present is not Being in the present—it is *thinking about* Being in the present. It is not something we can make a mood about. It is only something we can become aware of. When you're late for an appointment, caught in rush-hour traffic, or missing a deadline, catch your stressed state of mind and tune into the present. You will refresh yourself, save wasted energy, and be more effective.

> *Compared to what we ought to be, we are half awake.*
>
> —William James

When you become aware of the silent witness behind all your dynamic activity, Being is present. Gay Hendricks and Kate Ludeman write in *The Corporate Mystic*, "Corporate Mystics put a great deal of attention on learning to be in the present moment because they have found that this is the only place from which time can be expanded. If you are in the present—not caught up in regret about the past or anxiety about the future—time essentially becomes malleable." If we are always effective in the present moment, can effectiveness and fulfillment escape us?

• *Children at Play*

How deep is the meditation of a child at play? It is pure Being in action. The joy, energy, focus, spontaneity, and vibrancy of children can teach all of us the way to our goal. As John Steinbeck wrote, "Genius is a child chasing a butterfly up a mountain."

• *Love*

Love is the transcendental glue of the universe. Love unifies and connects everything. It is the vibration of Being in our lives. At the moment of pure love and appreciation, we transcend our limitations and connect with all there is. Love is the road to Being and the road from Being to the world.

• *Traumatic Events*

As difficult as dramatic changes in our lives are, the trauma of these events can shake us up so much that we cope by letting go of everything that seemed so important. In doing so, we can connect with something deeper within ourselves. Consider being more open to the vulnerability of unexpected changes as a pathway to our inner Self.

• *Inspirational Reading*

Reading the accounts of people on their journey to realization can be a helpful aid to us on our path. Even though we're reading about other people's experiences, the insights can be helpful and motivational as we progress. Sometimes they provide clarity and validation. Other times, we learn about an area of personal development we need to explore. Once in a while, we become inspired and awaken to our inner Self.

INSIGHTS • REFLECTIONS • COMMITMENTS •

BEING AND EXECUTIVE PRESENCE

Many of the executives I have coached over the years have what could be called *unconscious competence* when it comes to Being Mastery. It's unconscious because when I inquire into their experiences of inner silence supporting their effectiveness, they often give me a puzzled look. They may even get very uncomfortable and label such pursuits as "too esoteric or impractical." In spite of this lack of awareness, effective people often have a degree of competence in this area. Aspects of their lives reflect mastery of Being. Often they have what people call "executive presence"—a solid, confident, calm demeanor not easily shaken by external circumstances. Even though they may be experiencing some of the benefits of Being, they haven't made the connection consciously. Even though they are not fully aware of it, it is their Being, their inner presence, that inspires others to follow them.

Helping effective people to move their mastery of Being from unconscious competence to conscious competence is crucial. It is one of the most practical ways to impact effectiveness and fulfillment simultaneously. Devoid of conscious competence, our connection to the benefits of Being is haphazard and sporadic. As a result, we are likely to remain at our current level of realization and thereby limit our external performance. It's much like a naturally talented athlete who needs to become more conscious of his God-given talents and entire life situation to move to the next level. Mastery of Being allows us to play at an entirely new level—the player, the game, and the process of playing are all enhanced permanently. Jim Secord, CEO of Lakewood Publications, sees the practical benefits of grounding himself in these principles. Reflecting on the most challenging times in his career, he said, "Had I been unable to ground myself in spiritual principles and practices during the tough times, I wouldn't have been able to rise up to the challenges of leadership."

> *The soul will bring forth fruit exactly in the measure in which the inner life is developed in it. If there is no inner life, however great may be the zeal, the high intention, the hard work, no fruit will come forth.*
>
> —Charles de Foucald

LEADERSHIP BENEFITS OF BEING

As leaders, what are some of the practical benefits of bringing the awareness of Being to our conscious, everyday experience?

- Our inner calm attracts others to us. People are more comfortable with our increasingly peaceful yet dynamic presence. People tend to seek out our thoughtful advice and counsel.

- We are better equipped to deal with rapid change around us because we are more calm and centered within.

- Our drive for external success is enhanced by our awareness of deeper, more fundamental values. As a result, our external success has more meaning, context, and depth.

- We can solve tough, challenging problems more easily. Our minds can get above, below, and around seemingly difficult situations.

- The profound rest of Being gives us the ability to refresh ourselves and allows us to achieve more with less effort.

- More life balance is achieved because we have the energy and calmness to cope *dynamically* with life challenges. People sense our balance and trust our thoughtful, calm demeanor.

- We have the distinct sense that we are growing to become more uniquely and authentically ourselves. Qualities of character flow through us more often and more naturally.

If we want to *do more*, we first need to *be more*. As Emerson wrote, "We but half express ourselves, and are ashamed of that divine idea which each of us represents."

Take more time to reflect and to be. Since leaders lead by virtue of who they are, commit to expanding the depth of your character to its most essential level—Being.

INSIGHTS • REFLECTIONS • COMMITMENTS •

LEADERSHIP GROWTH COMMITMENTS

BEING MASTERY

Reflect on the learnings that have surfaced as you read this chapter. Identify three leadership growth commitments to enhance your connection with the peace and silence of Being. Then identify the potential obstacles, resources needed, and signs or measures of success.

1. Key Learnings:
   A. _____
   B. _____
   C. _____

2. Leadership Growth Commitments:
   A. _____
   B. _____
   C. _____

3. Resources Needed:
   A. _____
   B. _____
   C. _____

4. Potential Obstacles:
   A. _____
   B. _____
   C. _____

5. Timeline and Measures of Success:
   A. _____
   B. _____
   C. _____

FOUR POINTS OF AWARENESS FOR LEADING FROM BEING

Keep the following points in mind as you begin to master leading with calm dynamism.

*1. **Take Your Own Journey into Being:*** Find your own path to unfold Being. It's your road, and only you can travel it. Only you can judge what "vehicles" will help you on your journey. Consider meditation, prayer, reflection, music, nature, and any other "techniques" that seem to resonate with you. Start walking, and the journey is half over.

*2. **Resolve Life Challenges by Going to a Deeper Level:*** Problems rarely are solved on their own level. Learn to go to a deeper level to view things in a more comprehensive way. As your mind learns to settle down yet remain alert, the ability to sort through and to organize your life will be amazing. Understand the power of non-doing—those uniquely open, relaxed moments when the complex becomes simple, and the unsolvable is solved, easily and effortlessly.

*3. **Consider Learning to Meditate:*** At least consider the possibility of learning to meditate properly. It may be the best investment in your development you ever make. If you have a particularly strong resistance to spending time with yourself in reflection or meditation, then the need to do so is probably great. Allow the resistance to be there but still spend the time to do it. As you experience the benefits, the resistance will subside.

*4. **Integrate Some Reflection into Your Life:*** Getting on the path to Being involves

INSIGHTS • REFLECTIONS • COMMITMENTS •

committing to a lifestyle which values more solitude, reflection, and medita-tion. Take some "Being Breaks" by investing some time getting reacquainted with yourself. Enjoy the solitude. Go on some walks. Sort out your priorities. Experience the silence. Reducing the "noise" of normal living and spending time in nature can help you to reconnect. Try not to fill up all your time with speedboats and fishing. Don't just do some-thing—sit there! Enjoy the moonlight on the water, the cry of the loon, the scent of pine in the cool air, the crash of the waves. It will set-tle you down and bring you closer to yourself. But keep in mind this is not an end in itself. It is preparation for a more dynamic, master-ful life. It is not an escape, but rather a dis-covery—a process of finding and connecting with the gift of Life.

There is one means of procuring solitude which to me, and I apprehend all men, is effectual, and that is to go to a window and look at the stars. If they do not startle you and call you off from vulgar matters, I know not what will.

—Ralph Waldo Emerson

Being Mastery Summary

• *Take Your Own Journey into Being:* Getting on the path to self-discovery is your own very personal journey. Only you can decide what "vehicles" to take on your travels and how you want to get there. Start walking and enjoy both the process and the goal. If you want to achieve more as a leader, you first need to be more as a person.

• *Resolve Life Challenges by Going to a Deeper Level:* Problems are just opportunities seen from a limited vantage point. Learn to dive deeply within yourself to view your leadership and life challenges from a more comprehensive perspective. Leaders navigate from the depths of their Being; managers tend to cope with the waves on the surface.

• *Consider Learning to Meditate:* Learning to revitalize your mind and body is the inner basis for outer effectiveness. If you have a difficult time even considering the idea of learning some form of meditation practice, then remember the equation for personal and leadership development: resistance = need.

• *Integrate More Reflection into Your Life:* Taking the time to reduce the noise in your life allows you to hear and express the music in your soul. Profound insights and breakthrough ideas usually arise from the stillness of the leader's Being.

PATHWAY SIX: BALANCE MASTERY

Leading by Centering Our Life

Balance Mastery is the dynamic centering of our life to build resilience and to enhance effectiveness and fulfillment.

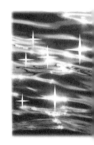

In preparing to write this book, I personally interviewed 53 CEOs and presidents of corporations. The purpose of these meetings was to solicit their views regarding our leadership models and to have them challenge our viewpoints. Additionally, we conducted research to discover which areas of mastery corporate leaders perceived as most relevant to their leadership effectiveness and which areas they viewed as the most challenging. The results of our survey were very clear-cut: 75 percent of the CEOs and presidents saw Personal Mastery as the most relevant to their leadership effectiveness. However, 92 percent of them selected Balance Mastery as the most challenging personally. Centering our life in the executive fast lane is a major balancing act.

Recently David, the CFO of a mid-size company, shared his wake-up call for balance with me. Returning from a two-week business trip, he was lifting his luggage out of the trunk of his car when his six-year-old son walked into the garage. Surprised by the unfamiliar sight of a man in his garage, the child ran back into the house screaming. His son actually mistook him for an intruder! In that moment, David knew it was time to re-enter all parts of his life.

CHALLENGES OF BALANCE FOR EXECUTIVES

Twelve months ago, I thought I had a balanced life pretty well figured out. On some levels I did as long as my life didn't change beyond my expectations. However, after nearly twenty years of steady, continuous growth, our executive coaching practice took a sudden leap forward, doubling in size over a very short period. With this sudden growth spurt, my life was wonderfully out of balance. I say "wonderfully" because I love the work so much. My problem was that it was too much of a good thing. I felt as if I was sitting at an incredible feast and I was not able to push away from the table. The "indigestion" of imbalance was causing harmful symptoms: strain in relationships, reduced energy level, diminished passion and physical stress. All this culminated in a couple of serious but manageable health issues. Unfortunately, the intensity of these symptoms had to become painful enough for me to pay attention. I definitely needed to re-master inner balance at an entirely new level. It took a few months of focused attention to take my life back. Over time, I was able to lay an even deeper foundation of balance for dealing with future growth challenges.

Slow down and enjoy life. It's not only the scenery you miss by going too fast—you also miss the sense of where you're going and why.

—Eddie Cantor

Although I feel more confident in Mastery of Balance now (particularly since I'm sitting on a beautiful beach at sunset as I write this), I know Balance Mastery is an ongoing challenge. It's a dynamic process. Once we are certain we have it mastered, the change in our life accelerates, and the process may need to be deepened once again.

WHAT HAPPENED TO THE LIFE OF LEISURE?

What happened to the life of leisure we were supposed to be living by now? Weren't we supposed to be working 20 to 30-hour work weeks with lots of leisure time on our hands? Not too long ago, futurists were predicting this as the natural outcome of our automated, computer age. Very few of us would say that our lives have become more leisurely. On the contrary, most people would say life is a constant flow of "have-to-dos" versus "want-to-dos." The pace of our lives has picked up considerably. Each new "convenience" like cellular phones, voice mail, and e-mail simultaneously delivers some "free time" with ten new things to do. Is it possible that doing more and more is not the answer? Is doing more in less time only going to increase our future demands? Is it possible that the answer is more fundamental, more internal than we previously thought?

Particularly in career settings, the potential for feeling overwhelmed is great. High-performing people naturally want to achieve more and more. High-performing organizations exhibit an insatiable desire to "pile" more and more responsibility on key people. On top of this, many companies, thinking they need to operate leaner and leaner, require fewer people to carry out more work. At precisely the time when people need to draw on greater resources of energy and drive, the reserves may be depleted. Finding ways to refresh, to revitalize and to balance ourselves has never been more crucial to our productivity and satisfaction.

BALANCE: NO LONGER A LUXURY, A MATTER OF SURVIVAL FOR LEADERS

In our executive coaching work, we often find personal balance to be a critical part of long-term effectiveness. An imbalanced, uncentered person is often an imbalanced, uncentered leader. If our internal compass is not in balance, it is difficult to find our own way much less point precise directions for others. If we are easily knocked off center by the waves of change, then someone else had better be navigating the ship. As John Hetterick, former President of Tonka and CEO of Rollerblade, shared with me, "Everyone around a leader knows when the leader is out of balance. People *hesitate* in the presence of an unbalanced leader. People *follow* a leader in balance."

INSIGHTS • REFLECTIONS • COMMITMENTS •

Unfortunately, many executives minimize the value of balancing their lifestyle to enhance leadership performance. A while ago, I met with a senior executive in a major corporation who was keenly interested in our *Executive to Leader Institute*. He was extremely engaged by how we integrated the personal mastery, leadership mastery, interpersonal mastery, and career mastery aspects of the process. However, he was totally against including balance mastery as part of his program. He strongly objected to the relevance of it. "What does having a more balanced life have to do with my leadership performance anyway?" Because I knew this person's reputation for blowing up at people for insignificant things, I knew he needed more balance, and I needed to press the point. However, even after a lengthy discussion on how being more balanced and centered directly affects how we lead, as well as our ability to cope with the endless demands of highly responsible positions, he was still resistant. Rather than press him further, I gave him some materials and suggested we get together in a few days. The meeting never happened. The 42-year-old executive died of a massive heart attack two days later. Balancing our lifestyle is not a luxury, it is a necessity. As leaders, balance allows us first to survive and second to thrive.

He who bends to himself a Joy doth the winged life destroy. But he who kisses the Joy as it flies lives in eternity's sunrise.

—William Blake

WHAT HEALTHY, PRODUCTIVE 100-YEAR-OLDS CAN TEACH LEADERS

A five-year study, completed by Dr. Leonard Poon of the University of Georgia, revealed some interesting principles regarding mastery of balance. In his study of 97 active, productive people over one hundred years of age, he found that they had mastered four common characteristics:

1. *Optimism:* They tended to have a positive view of the past and future. They were not dominated by worry or negativity.

2. *Engagement:* They were actively involved in life. They were not passive observers, allowing life to pass them by.

3. *Mobility:* They stayed active physically. One person was an aerobics instructor; most walked or gardened daily.

4. *Adaptability to Loss:* They had an extraordinary ability to stay balanced by adapting to and accepting change and loss. Even though most of them had lost their families and friends, they still had a zest for living.

The study also uncovered one interesting surprise. These 100-year-olds tended to eat whatever they wanted. In fact, most of them had a high-fat, high-calorie diets. What was their secret to a healthy lifestyle? They were happy, involved, active, balanced people. They appeared to have mastered the joy of balanced living.

BALANCE IS A DYNAMIC PROCESS

Balance Mastery is not a static, rigid process; it is a dynamic reconciliation of extremes. When we are balanced, we are not stationary. On the contrary, Balance Mastery is the type of centered fluidity that lets us go in any direction with ease and agility. It is not a rigid, heavy, immobile or restricted process. Being centered means we can recover our balance even in the midst of action. Too often people think about balancing their lives as a mechanistic process. First we separate our career, personal, family, emotional, and spiritual lives into distinct pieces and then try to balance the parts on a scale. Managing the entire dynamic is the key, not manipulating the separate pieces. We need to locate the dynamics that run through all the pieces and then influence our balance at that level. Mastery of Balance is about finding ways to connect with our center so we can deal with all the dynamics outside. As we unfold more inner balance, we can do more with ease. Actually, when we are centered we can shoulder more weight with less effort because

INSIGHTS • REFLECTIONS • COMMITMENTS •

As a silversmith sifts dust from silver, remove your own imbalances little by little.

—The Dhammapada

we are centered below the balance point. Finding ways to center ourselves from the inside out is the key to Balance Mastery.

THE TEN SIGNS OF BALANCE MASTERY

So what are some of the signs of Balance Mastery?

- Smooth, abundant energy
- Ability to focus deeply
- Internally driven motivation
- Optimism
- Fulfilling, intimate relationships
- Creativity and innovation
- Vitality and enthusiasm
- Little or no usage of caffeine, nicotine, alcohol, or drugs
- Achievement with ease
- Optimal productivity

THE TEN SIGNS OF IMBALANCE

What are some of the signs of lack of balance?

- Nervous, manic energy
- Wandering, unfocused mind
- Externally driven motivation
- Negativity
- Strain in relationships
- Dullness, lack of inspiration
- Depression and fatigue
- Regular usage of caffeine, nicotine, alcohol, or drugs
- Achievement via strain and effort
- Less than optimal productivity

NATURE'S BALANCING ACT: REST AND ACTIVITY

How do we go about finding more balance in our lives? The best model for balance exists in nature. All balance in nature unfolds through alternate cycles of rest and activity. The cycles of day and night and the seasonal cycles constantly balance a rest phase with an active phase. Nature expresses its vitality in the active phase. Nature reconnects with its vitality in the rest phase. Each phase interacts in just the right combination to achieve dynamic balance. Our lives are similar with one major difference: We get to choose the quantity and quality of activity, as well as the quantity and quality of rest. When we choose inappropriately, our life is out of whack. When we choose well, we experience balance and vitality. Nature lets us choose freely, but she also gives us immediate feedback on how well we have chosen. As we learn to listen better, our balance and vitality increase.

INSIGHTS • REFLECTIONS • COMMITMENTS •

Most imbalances in our society come from two major sources: We tend to overdo our activity, and we tend to underdo our rest. The formula for most of us to foster more balance in our lives usually involves two things:

1. Improve the quality of our activity and reduce the quantity somewhat.
2. Improve the quality and quantity of our rest.

THE TEN BALANCE POINTS OF LEADERS

What are some ways to satisfy both of these requirements? Although there could be many others, I've found ten points of Balance Mastery that can help center our lives in an integrated, holistic way:

- Be on-purpose, but be aware
- Learn to exercise with ease
- Deal with life-damaging habits
- Avoid taking yourself so seriously
- Develop mind-body awareness
- Manage stress more effectively

- Nurture your close relationships
- Simplify your life
- Take real vacations
- Integrate more reflection and introspection into your lifestyle

Let's take a close look at each of these balance points:

One can never consent to creep when one feels an impulse to soar.

—Helen Keller

1. Be On-Purpose, But Be Aware: Of all the points of balance, discovering our purpose is one of the most important. It is our centered position of strength. When we are on-purpose, it is most difficult for others to knock us off-balance. So often, while we are caught up in the activity of our lives, we seldom ask ourselves, "Why?" As Thoreau reflected on our imbalanced manner of living, he wrote, "It is not enough to be busy; so are the ants. The question is, what are we busy about?" Rather than simply amassing a great pile of achievements or experiences, our life can be about burning a passionate fire that illuminates our way. But we have to be careful. As our passionate purpose burns strongly, our devotion to it also can cause us to throw ourselves out of balance. We become so single-minded about our mission, we can begin to ignore our rest, physical needs, or relationships. Therefore, be purposeful but beware: Purpose is a balance point from which we can fall.

I'm often asked by people about my ability to be so "disciplined." People conjecture, "Owning a consulting business, writing books, doing triathlons, having close relationships, meditating daily—how do you do it? You must be very disciplined." I'm always taken aback. I don't believe in discipline. Discipline is forcing yourself to do something you really don't want to do, a surefire prescription for failure and rigidity. If people said to me, "You must really love what you do. You must feel passionate and purposeful about your life," I would probably be a little embarrassed, but at the same time, I would feel at home with their comment. Purpose is the balance point that allows us to achieve multiple goals with ease.

2. Learning to Exercise with Ease: You may be surprised to hear this from someone who has participated in triathlons for years, but we are killing ourselves with our unenlightened approaches to exercise. Unknowingly, most people don't exercise, they punish themselves. Many get so disconnected from their body that they mistakenly associate the fatigue they feel with a "high." The "No Pain, No Gain" mentality usually creates more fatigue, stress, injury, and imbalance than any real type of fitness. We really need to re-think exercise.

We need to go to a deeper level and ask ourselves, "What is the *purpose* of exercise?" Certainly losing weight, looking good, or setting a new personal record are some superficial purposes, but not the most profound, compelling ones. If you are a professional athlete, the purpose of exercise may be to express your spirit in the physical realm as no one else has done before.

Insights • Reflections • Commitments •

Most of us, however, are not professional athletes, and we need to find a meaning of fitness for us. Isn't that meaning closer to the Greek ideal of mind-body integration? Isn't it about rejuvenating ourselves, bringing more vitality, energy, and joy of movement into our lives? For me, the purpose of exercise is to strengthen our vehicle so it can support more effectively our overall life purpose. It's about enjoying the happiness of Being expressed in our physical nature. A pretty heady framework for push-ups, dumbbells, and sweaty runs, isn't it?

Some of our more driven executive clients proudly tell us they "exercise *every day* without fail." When we ask them if they enjoy it, they look a bit confused and respond, "Well no, but I do it *every day*, anyway!" If it takes discipline to run, then find something else that you enjoy doing.

Fitness has to be fun. If it is not play, there will be no fitness. Play, you see, is the process. Fitness is merely the product.

—George Sheehan

Activities you enjoy bring balance. Activities you dislike create imbalance. The joy of the activity itself is as health-giving as the aerobic effect. Besides, if you don't enjoy it, you will either "succeed" in becoming a more rigid person or you will quit it eventually anyway. What we love, we stay with. Find ways that you love to move your physical being.

The most enlightened perspective I have found on exercise is in the book *Body, Mind and Sport* by Dr. John Douillard. Using ancient techniques of mind-body integration, he guides people through a program to experience the "zone," the exercise high, every time. People start to truly enjoy exercise as they find their minds deeply composed in the midst of dynamic physical activity. Within this new paradigm, Douillard writes, "This gives us a new, uniquely challenging fitness goal. We're no longer content to see how much we can do; we want to know how effortlessly we can do it!" You may want to read Douillard's book to get a complete picture. In the meantime, consider some of these suggestions for more enlightened exercise:

- Find an activity (or activities) you love.

- Set the uncompromising goal that you are going to feel good throughout the exercise program. If you feel any strain, go more slowly. If you lose your breath or cannot comfortably hold a conversation with a training partner, slow down.

- Breathe in and out *through your nose* the entire workout. If you have to breathe through your mouth, you're straining, so slow down.

- Always warm up by walking or very slowly beginning your activity for 10–15 minutes before you start exercising.

- Do light stretching only after you are warmed up—stretch, never strain. Consider incorporating gentle, effective stretching into your routine.

- Maintain an awareness of your body and how it feels during the entire workout. If you do not feel comfortable throughout the workout, slow down or stop until you do.

- Walk for 5–10 minutes to cool down. Do more light stretching.

- Start gauging your fitness by how good you feel *during* and *after* the activity, not by how hard you worked yourself or how far or fast you went.

INSIGHTS • REFLECTIONS • COMMITMENTS •

If you follow this process regularly, you will enjoy the exercise session and remain more balanced. Most athletes are always on the verge of fatigue, illness, and injury, so they are always somewhat imbalanced. Exercise with ease. You will improve your fitness, balance, and quality of life, all in one process.

If you are having trouble finding time to keep active, remember, Thomas Jefferson believed in getting two hours of exercise every day. If someone who wrote the Declaration of Independence, became President, and was Secretary of State could find two hours a day, you can find 20–30 minutes a few times a week! Check with a physician before you begin any exercise program.

3. Deal with Life-Damaging Habits: Poor lifestyle choices account for more misery, suffering, death, and imbalance in our society than any other single or multiple cause.

The choice to smoke cigarettes, for instance, is the cause of more than 420,000 deaths each year in the United States. That's seven times higher than the number of Americans who died in the entire Vietnam War. This represents only one lifestyle choice! What about the abuse of alcohol and drugs, as well as poor choices in the areas of food, relationships, and exercise? It has been estimated that more than 70 percent of all disease has a basis in poor lifestyle decisions. It may sound dramatic, but lifestyle decisions can lead you in one of two directions—life or death.

The human body is the best picture of the human soul.

—Ludwig Wittgenstein

It's hard to fathom how much imbalance life-damaging habits cause. Most of us don't engage in behaviors to harm ourselves. The problem is that we have mistaken certain habits for happiness. We unknowingly exchange a short-term fix for long-term damage. How do we retreat from behaviors we know are hurting us? Mark Twain captured the challenge of moving away from certain behaviors when he said, "Habit is habit, and not to be flung out of the window, but coaxed downstairs a step at a time." The steps for coaxing them downstairs are:

- *Admit that the habit is damaging to you and possibly others.* Go deeply into all the negative effects this habit is having on you. Until you acknowledge the problem, you won't have any genuine motivation to change.

- *Get professional or peer support to help you.* It's unlikely you can do it on your own, or you would have done it already.

- *Find positive behaviors to replace the old addictions.* As the old proverb goes, "You can more easily drive out a tough nail with another nail." Replace smoking with exercise, desserts with fruit, coffee with herbal teas, and so forth.

- *Continually repeat the first three steps* if the habits take hold again or new ones appear.

Habits that involve stimulants like coffee and nicotine are particularly indicative of lack of balance. The need for artificial stimulants typically is masking the deep fatigue within. To help yourself as you ease out of these particular habits, additional rest and meditation greatly accelerate the balancing process.

4. Avoid Taking Yourself So Seriously: Humor and lightheartedness balance mind, body, and spirit. The more rigid and self-centered we are, the more out of balance we become. Proverbs 17:22 captures the essence of this principle: "A cheerful heart is good medicine." Imagine yourself in your most secure, strong moments. Aren't these the times you can laugh at yourself and observe life in a playful manner? Letting go of our own rigid, external mask brings balance and joy into our life. Harriet Rochlin wrote, "Laughter can be more satisfying than honor; more precious than money; more heart-cleansing than prayer."

INSIGHTS • REFLECTIONS • COMMITMENTS •

Taking ourselves too seriously can go very deeply. Years ago a friend of mine set up a lecture event for a well-known teacher of Hatha Yoga. It was a big event at a university with hundreds of people in attendance. In an effort to consider every imaginable detail, my friend kindly brought the teacher a glass of ice water. The teacher snapped at him, "Don't you know that a Yogi does not drink water with ice in it?" My friend calmly responded, "I didn't know that. Did you know that a Yogi usually has a blissful, balanced mind?"

Treat life like a play. Be serious about the plot, your fellow actors, and doing it well. But don't take yourself too seriously. In the broader scheme of things, it's just a role in the cosmic play.

Have you ever seen an energetic dog let loose onto an open field—the pure joy and exhilaration of its run, stretching its boundaries, expressing its freedom? It's a wonderful thing to witness. Maybe it's time to set your seriousness aside and take a joyous run into your open field!

Learn to unclutter your mind. Learn to simplify your work. As you rely less and less on knowing just what to do, your work will become more direct and powerful. You will discover that the quality of your consciousness is more potent than any technique or theory or interpretation.

—John Heider

5. Develop Mind-Body Awareness: Most of us are stuck in our heads. We need to pay more attention to our body's messages. Our body reflects everything that's going on in our lives. It is our primary feedback mechanism to reveal the positive or negative impact of our thoughts, emotions, or choices. Start listening to the wisdom of the body. It speaks through energy. *Translation:* Do more of that! It talks through fatigue. *Translation:* Cut down on that and give me more rest! It sends painful messages. *Translation:* I've been warning you gently, but since you ignored me, I will talk a lot louder—stop doing that! Developing awareness of how the mind affects the body and how the body affects the mind is a crucial skill. Fostering mind-body awareness can be one of our most healing and balancing inside-out competencies.

6. Manage Stress More Effectively: Stress is a totally subjective reality. If two people are stressed the same way, one may collapse and the other may thrive on the challenging opportunity. Stress is determined by how we process our world. I recently experienced this firsthand while on a consulting trip in London and Paris. I arrived at the airport only to find the terminal jammed and the flight delayed. In the grander scheme of things, it was not an earth-shattering event. Unfortunately, many people in the terminal were behaving (i.e., processing their world) as if a major disaster had happened. Once we boarded, I went to the restroom, and since it was occupied, I stood outside and collected myself. Suddenly, inside the tiny restroom, I heard a tremendous struggle going on with crashes and pounding noises. My first thought was that someone was venting their frustration. Then, just as I was about to get some help, the door flew open and a head popped out. It was a severely physically handicapped man with crutches attached to each arm and paralyzed legs that he only could swing around to follow his contorted upper body. In the midst of his noisy struggle to exit the cramped quarters, he looked up at me with a knowing smile and said, "I'm just a butterfly freeing myself from my cocoon!" It was a wonderful moment that I will never forget. If only we all could "process our world" with such dignity, heart, and balance.

One of my colleagues, Janet Feldman, has developed a solid framework to "process our world" by discerning between three things:

- What Can We *Control?*
- What Can We *Influence?*
- What Must We *Accept?*

Each time you face a stressful situation or event, achieve balance by asking yourself, "What can I *control* in this situation? What can I do to *influence* this situation? What do I have to *accept* here?" Distress is usually the by-product of wasting energy by trying to control things we can only influence or accept, or accepting things we could influence or control. Take action on what you can control or influence and let go of what you have to accept.

This simple formula, along with the principles of Being Mastery, can be very helpful as you face difficult circumstances. There is no greater immunity to stress than connection to your inner self.

INSIGHTS • REFLECTIONS • COMMITMENTS •

7. *Nurture Your Close Relationships:* Few things in life can instantaneously balance us as quickly as love. A difficult, stressful day quickly can be put in perspective by the innocence and pure love of a child. Few people could help us to sort out a difficult situation like a supportive spouse or friend. Close relationships can be our anchors in the sea of change. But this "closeness" does not come *from* others to us. It originates as intimacy with ourselves first. We can only give what we have. If our emotional bank account is low, no spending is possible. So the key is to develop emotional equity with oneself first. Then we will be able to be there for others in their time of need. Likewise, they will be there for us in our time of need. Sooner or later, we will need to take an "emotional loan" from one of our close relationships to balance our life account.

> *The moment of victory is much too short to live for that and nothing else.*
>
> —Martina Navratilova

To help him understand the value of life's most essential relationships, a CEO's spouse advised him, "A few years after you leave your job most people will forget you, but your family will always remember you."

8. *Simplify Your Life:* Will Rogers certainly captured how we can unnecessarily complicate our lives when he wrote, "Too many people spend money they haven't earned, to buy things they don't need, to impress the people they don't like." The more we have been living from the "outside in," the more complicated and imbalanced our lives become. The harder we strive to improve *the things* in our lives, the more complex our lives become. As Lily Tomlin has said, "The trouble with the rat race is that even if you win, you're still the rat!"

What are the underlying principles for simplifying life? Sort out *needs* versus *wants* and connect with your purpose. Understanding and living our lives consistent with what is really important to us is the process needed to get back to basics. Ask yourself three crucial questions: Is it possible that your focus on satisfying your wants (versus needs) is complicating your life unnecessarily? Is your pursuit of wants taking you away from the life you really hope to live? Are you living on-purpose? If any of the answers is no, don't panic. Feel relieved that you finally see things more clearly, and remind yourself that you don't have to change everything immediately. Take some small steps. Start to rearrange your finances. Make more values-based purchasing decisions. In *The Law of Success*, Paramahansa Yogananda once wrote, "The problem in life is not possessions. The question is, do the possessions support your purpose?" Commit to the process of sorting out your *wants* versus *needs*. Begin to simplify your life by making more choices that support the vision of the life you really want to live.

9. Take Real Vacations: How often have we gone on a vacation only to return more tired and worn-out than when we left? As fun as it is to expand our boundaries by experiencing new places, does it provide us with the restful balance we need? Instead of "emptying our bucket," we fill it up with even more stimulation and activity. Why not try a real vacation next time? Why not get some real rest to provide some life perspective? Some of the best examples of real vacations:

INSIGHTS • REFLECTIONS
• COMMITMENTS •

- *Go to a health spa.* Taking a few days for good food, massage, and rest can turn you around. If you can't actually travel to a spa, consider creating your own spa by unplugging the TV, getting more rest, taking a long walk, getting a massage, and journaling your latest aspirations.

- *Go on a retreat.* Transform your perspective via the gentle, quiet routine of a spiritual or personal retreat. Don't go on a retreat that fills up your day with activities. To advance, you may need to retreat first.

- *Go on a vacation by yourself.* If your spouse or significant other is secure enough to let you go, it can be a great way to reconnect. There must be a cabin somewhere you'd love to go.

- *Stay at home for a week.* Some of my best, most refreshing vacations have been staying at home. If you travel a lot, this can be the best way to get away.

Try one of these options for your next vacation and recognize the balancing effects over a period of months.

What is without periods of rest will not endure.

—Ovid

10. Integrate More Reflection and Introspection into Your Lifestyle: As leaders, how often do we take time to reflect? In spite of the fact that we are the strategic thinkers behind our organizations, how often do we really step back to re-think ourselves, our lives, and our organizations? On this subject Larry Perlman, Chairman and CEO of Ceridian, explained, "I would rather have a senior executive go on a weekend of personal reflection than go to another leadership seminar. Leadership is not about learning theory. It's about finding out how you are going to bring yourself into your work and into your life to make a contribution."

If we aspire to *do more*, then we must *be more*. Taking time to reflect, taking time to be, is crucial to leaders. It is the still point that everything else revolves around. The more dynamic and effective we want to be in outer life, the more still and composed we need to be within. The more dynamic the system in nature, the more silent the interior. The eye of the hurricane is silent and still—the center of all the energy. The ancient text, *The Bhagavad Gita*, captured the essence of balance, "Established in Being, perform action." This is what real balance is all about. Consider integrating meditation, reflection, prayer, reading, journaling, music, nature, and any other process that brings more balance and awareness to your dynamic life.

REFLECTION

BALANCE MASTERY

Leading by Centering Our Life

1. What can you do to improve the quality of your activity or reduce the quantity to bring more balance into your lifestyle?

2. What can you do to improve the quality of rest to revitalize yourself?

3. What habits do you need to replace with more positive behaviors?

4. What are your internal motivators for achieving more balance?

5. What are your external motivators for achieving more balance?

6. What is your vision of the more balanced life you want to live?

7. How is your pursuit of wants (versus needs) unnecessarily complicating your life and taking you away from your life vision?

8. Reflect on what choices would connect you more precisely with your life vision.

LEADERSHIP GROWTH COMMITMENTS

BALANCE MASTERY

Reflect on the learnings that have surfaced as you read this chapter. Identify three leadership growth commitments to enhance balance in your life. Then identify the potential obstacles, resources needed, and signs or measures of success.

1. Key Learnings:
A. _____
B. _____
C. _____

2. Leadership Growth Commitments:
A. _____
B. _____
C. _____

3. Resources Needed:
A. _____
B. _____
C. _____

4. Potential Obstacles:
A. _____
B. _____
C. _____

5. Timeline and Measures of Success:
A. _____
B. _____
C. _____

BALANCE MASTERY SUMMARY

- *Choose Wisely:* Every lifestyle choice adds or depletes energy from you as a leader. Replacing life-damaging habits with life-giving ones provides the resilience needed to help you lead more effectively.

- *Be On-Purpose:* Connecting with your purpose can center and balance you as a leader. However, be careful—single-minded career passion can throw you out of balance in other parts of your life.

- *Rest and Reflect More:* Balance your dynamic leadership demands with more rest and reflection. If you want to do more, then you need to be more.

- *Exercise for Enjoyment:* Find activities you love and learn to appreciate the effortless joy of movement. Adopt a "No Joy, No Gain" exercise mentality. Build your fitness level to support your stamina as a leader.

- *Simplify Your Life:* Evaluate what is essential in the context of your values, purpose, and character. Ask yourself, "Are these choices adding to my purpose? Are these choices character-driven or persona-driven?"

- *Loosen Up:* Play creates balance. Stop taking yourself so seriously. Nothing is more uninspiring than a boring, rigid leader. Leaders who are fun, playful, and joyful tend to attract and retain committed, motivated, energetic people.

PATHWAY SEVEN: ACTION MASTERY

Leading as a Whole Person

Action Mastery is the ongoing commitment to creating value through enhanced authenticity and self-expression.

Leading as a whole person means integrating and focusing the diverse learnings gained in each mastery area, deepening authenticity, heightening self-expression, and increasing the value you can create as a leader. Action Mastery is the ongoing commitment to pull together all of our inner resources in order to go beyond what we thought was possible. As Pearl S. Buck wrote, "All things are possible until they are proved impossible—and even the impossible may only be so, as of now."

GOING BEYOND OUR LIMITS

As I reflect on Action Mastery and about how much untapped potential we all have, I'm reminded of another experience I had a few years ago on Lake Superior. (I know you're thinking, "Can't that guy just stay off that darned lake!")

A friend and I had been staying for a few days in a small, rustic cabin on a cliff overlooking the lake. Each day we waited for a calm morning to explore the caves and hidden beaches accessible only by water. But the water each day was too rough to venture out. On the fourth day, the lake was totally calm—not a ripple to be seen. With great excitement, we packed up our gear and headed out onto the placid, smooth sea.

We were thrilled to be gliding atop the water on such a perfect day. Peering over the sides of our craft into the chilly depths, we could see the beautiful yet ominous world that stirred both our excitement and vulnerability. Seeing the gigantic slabs of rock and boulders polished smooth over thousands of years gave us a fresh perspective. My friend fantasized about draining the lake and exploring the mountains and valleys below. Our canoeing was effortless and smooth. Our first real clearing from the cliffs and rocks came about five miles down the lake at a beautiful old lodge. We decided to stay in the clearing and take a leisurely rest. We laid back in the canoe and caught some sunshine for 10 or 15 minutes. Suddenly a cold wind (not a cool breeze) passed over us. I perked up and noticed the flag at the lodge standing straight out—a warning signal. We jumped up, grabbed our paddles, and decided to head back.

> *We delude ourselves into thinking that it is safer to stay in the zone of the predictable. This, however, can be a bad bargain, especially if we want to go all the way to full success in life. . . . The moment we choose to stay in the predictable zone is the moment we sign our death warrant as a creative individual.*
>
> —Gay Hendricks and
> Kate Ludeman

The lake gradually mustered energy. At first, we joked back and forth about the waves and how fun it was. About a mile and a half out, the jokes were over. We were caught in the wild waves of Superior. Because the waves were breaking so high, the most dangerous areas were closest to the rocky cliffs of the shoreline. We had no choice; we had to keep going out further into the lake for "safety." The waves were so high that my friend's head dropped beneath the top of them. As we descended over them, the canoe would land with a loud slap.

Realizing we were in a life-or-death situation, we encouraged each other (sometimes in not-so-calm voices) and affirmed our resolve to get through this arduous challenge. While coping with the wild waves, I lost my life preserver, which hooked itself under our canoe. It not only slowed us down, but if we capsized . . . you get the picture. We just kept going. We got our second winds, third winds, fourth winds. After a while we were definitely in a "zone"—a calm, focused place amidst the raging waters. In fact we got so absorbed that after four hours of paddling, we actually passed our cabin! Overcome with joy and relief, we glided into our little cove—our safe haven—and collapsed on the rocks like two exhausted beached whales.

That evening, as we reflected on the wild day, we were astounded at the levels of inner strength and potentiality we had. We passed our limits many times. We transcended them so completely that we went to a place of effortlessness, totally unexpected by either of us. How much farther could we have gone? I don't know. All I know is that we went several times farther than we thought was possible.

What is our potentiality for achievement from the inside-out? Does life really have infinite possibilities as the great sages and thinkers have said throughout history? Is our world really a field of all possibilities, teaming with life, energy, and seemingly endless options? Or, does our life have a more limited horizon of success and possibility?

Researchers in the neurophysiology of the brain are beginning to give us some profound insights into our real potentiality. Using conservative estimates, researchers have projected that there are 100 trillion neuron junctions in the human brain. That means that our possible mental states are more than the total number of atoms in the universe! Think about that. Our brain potentially can find more possibilities than there are atoms in the universe. Is it possible for us to comprehend infinity? Maybe. Is our field of possibilities vastly larger than we think? Definitely.

Few would question the far reaches of our potentiality. The real question is, "How well are we using this potential?" Are we playing the concerto of life with one finger? William James wrote, "Most people live, whether physically, intellectually, or morally, in a very restricted circle of their potential being. They make use of a very small portion of their possible consciousness, and of their soul's resources in general, much like a

INSIGHTS • REFLECTIONS • COMMITMENTS •

man who, out of his whole bodily organism should opt into a habit of using and moving only his little finger."

Leadership from the Inside Out is about playing the song of our life with depth, grace, and passion. How can we ensure that we don't have only an occasional beautiful concert, but gradually become the harmonious melody itself?

> *Genius is the power to*
> *labor better and more*
> *availably than others.*
>
> —Ralph Waldo Emerson

Not long ago, two executives were referred to us for leadership coaching. They both had about the same level of compensation, and they both had about 20 years of uninterrupted success with *Fortune* 500 companies. They both excelled on the job. They both also needed to work on their leadership and interpersonal effectiveness if they wanted to continue to advance in their organizations. Each approached their development in dramatically different ways. One person was open to learning and willing to commit to the growth process from the inside out. The other person felt that he already "had it all figured out."

At the start of the coaching, they both exhibited reasonable willingness. After a few days, one lost enthusiasm as he got closer to some real feedback on his style and personality. He began to regard the process as "lots of work" and would say, "I'm not sure how relevant it is." He began to miss some appointments. As he pulled back, he began to speculate if the program was "worth it." He became increasingly skilled at fulfilling his prophecy and at rationalizing his lack of benefit.

The other person stayed with the program. He threw himself into every coaching session. He indulged himself in the self-exploration. He listened to the feedback and looked for ways to understand and to apply the information to his career and life in a relevant manner. He explored deeply his core meaning and purpose. He projected a new vision for his life. He committed to more balanced, healthful living. He began to read and reflect more. He started a journal. He shared his insights with others. He began to open up with people at work. He began to admit his strengths and weaknesses to others and to ask for their help. He stayed the course. He became a very effective, empowering leader. He got onto the path to *Leadership from the Inside Out.* Within a year, he was promoted to president of the corporation.

The other person? He was outplaced six months later. He continued the same pattern of not taking responsibility and projecting his limitations externally. He probably still blames his former company for his misfortunes.

EARNING A LIVING OR FEEDING A COMMUNITY?

INSIGHTS • REFLECTIONS • COMMITMENTS •

As you can see, similar circumstances can yield vastly different interpretations and results. Early in the 1900s, three people were working in a field on a large, productive farm. A passerby asked each one what they were doing. The first person responded, "What a dumb question—I'm tilling the soil!" The second said, "Just earning a living." The third person, eyes sparkling with purpose proclaimed, "I'm feeding the entire community!" All three were engaged in the same activity, but only one had comprehended skill in action. Only one was achieving with purpose. How often as leaders are we simply "tilling the soil" or "earning a living"? How often are our actions serving a higher need and "feeding the community"?

Too often as leaders we get lost in our actions. Consumed in our endless pursuit of results, we rarely question, "Why?" Achieving another billion dollars in sales or increasing shareholder value is the modern equivalent of "earning a living." It is less often equivalent to the action mastery required to "feed the community."

Bill George, Chairman and CEO of Medtronic, appreciates how "feeding the community" drives the results. In his words, "I believe that it is very difficult for employees to identify with a corporate mission of 'maximizing shareholder value.' Our purpose is to 'maximize patient value.' Our real bottom line is the 1.5 million patients who were restored to full life and health last year by Medtronic products." It's important to note that these words are spoken by the CEO of a company that has increased shareholder value from $1.1 billion to $15 billion in eight years. Medtronic has stayed focused on creating value, on "feeding the community," and their incredible results are driven by this purposeful mission. Few people at Medtronic would say they are "just earning a living." Most would respond enthusiastically that they are "restoring people to health."

> *Just be what you are and speak from your guts and heart—it's all a man has.*
>
> —Hubert Humphrey

As you can see, "feeding the community" is not just a great idea—it is action connected to purpose and vision. While authentic leadership is grounded in who we are, it creates value through our action. As important as authenticity and self-expression are, value and contribution are created through action. However, *Leadership from the Inside Out* is not action for the sake of action. It is not the mindless pursuit of results without regard for long-term consequences. It is skill in action—action originating from deep within the leader's character and purpose. Action Mastery is the process of integrating and applying our diverse inner resources as we create outer value.

THREE CORE PRINCIPLES UNDERLYING ACTION MASTERY

What are the principles that can guide mastery of skillful action for a leader? Paralleling our definition of leadership—*authentic self-expression that creates value*—there are three core principles underlying Action Mastery:

1. Action Mastery Principle One: Authenticity: There is no "inside" coming "out" without authenticity. Authenticity is the foundation, the platform, for *Leadership from the Inside Out.* Action without authenticity can actually create more problems for a leader than doing nothing at all. Bob James, President of

Allianz of North America, recently shared with me, "There is no such thing as leadership without the two 'T's': Truth and Trust. These principles are the essence, the spiritual foundation, which supports all effective leadership."

The need for leaders to face honestly all aspects of themselves is crucial. Personal characteristics that are denied, underdeveloped, or unseen by the leaders are perceived clearly by everyone around them. It's inescapable. Whatever we don't see in ourselves, others do. Facing all facets of ourselves is the basis for others to trust us as authentic people and leaders.

INSIGHTS • REFLECTIONS
• COMMITMENTS •

One of the finest examples of authenticity I've come across is from the Toro Company. Following a peak of unparalleled expansion and development in 1979, the company faced a drastic fall in demand for its snow-removal equipment from 1980 to 1981, due to two consecutive years of virtually no snowfall in any of the world's snowbelts. Combined with a worldwide recession and interest rates of 20 percent, the firm lost $13 million, its first loss since 1945. Sales fell sharply: 50 percent over two years. As a result, the company was top-heavy in management, had excessive staffs, and had corporate overhead rates out of line with competitors. Morale hit an all-time low.

In 1981, the entire line management team was terminated except one person—Ken Melrose. Ken was made president as the company was on the verge of bankruptcy. After the company was reduced in size from 4200 employees to 1800, Ken brought everyone together and addressed them with openness and authenticity, "We're in a very severe crisis, and you're wondering what went wrong. Well, management has let you down, and the entire management team is gone except me. If you have to blame someone, then blame me. If you want to be part of the solution then join me, and we'll bring this company back from the ashes."

Authenticity is the single most important quality of leadership. You cannot "get authentic" by delivering a great speech. It is demonstrated day-to-day through thousands of micro-behaviors.

—Bob Kidder

As the remaining people at Toro sensed, this was not just a great speech, it was the beginning of a cultural transformation. It took four years of trust-building and hard work, but Toro turned the entire business around. Interestingly, in 1991, Toro hit another tough year, but it only took one year to recover—the authenticity and trust were now an integral part of the culture able to deal with crisis in a more resilient manner.

What would have happened if Ken Melrose had made excuses instead of facing everyone with authenticity? Morale and performance would have fallen even lower. Melrose's courage and candor opened up the culture and were the glue to rebuild trust in the organization. As Ken shared with me, "Allowing our humanness to show unleashes the power of authentic leadership."

In every moment we are leading, life is attempting to teach us. The principle variable is how open or closed we are. I am amazed to meet so many leaders who view their role as "having all the answers." They don't realize that they are in a closed state of being. Shifting our awareness from one of knowing to one of learning is the receptiveness required for authenticity. One of the most enlightened CEOs I know shared with me, "People tell me I'm so smart and strategic. I'm really not. What I am is open. I am rarely afraid to not know." When we lack this type of emotional security, we unknowingly limit the flow of authenticity.

When you face your next challenge, ask yourself, "What is life attempting to teach me? What am I resisting being open to? What can I acknowledge not knowing or understanding?" Asking these questions can open up the floodgates of learning and authenticity.

Being authentic is an endless journey. We are always on the path to revealing ourselves more authentically. Nathaniel Branden, author of *Six Pillars of Self-Esteem*, wrote in the March 1997 issue of *Personal Excellence* magazine:

> We live a lie when we misrepresent the reality of our experience or the truth of our being. I am living a lie when I pretend a love I do not feel; when I pretend an indifference I do not feel; when I present myself as more than I am; when I say I am angry, and the truth is I am afraid; when I pretend to be helpless, and the truth is I am manipulative; when I deny and conceal my excitement about life; when I affect a blindness that denies my awareness; when I affect a knowledge I do not possess; when I laugh when I need to cry; when I spend unnecessary time with people I dislike; when I present myself as the embodiment of values I do not feel or hold; when I am kind to everyone except those I profess to love; when I fake beliefs to win acceptance; when I fake modesty; when I fake arrogance; when I allow my silence to imply agreement with convictions I do not share.

INSIGHTS • REFLECTIONS • COMMITMENTS •

Start to build an awareness of the times you have been authentic. What was going on? Why did you have the courage to be yourself? How can you replicate this experience?

Reflect on the times you have been less than authentic, the times you have withheld your real thoughts or feelings, the times you have placed an overly positive or negative spin on something. What was going on? What fears were holding you back from fully expressing yourself? How can you apply these learnings?

2. Action Mastery Principle Two: Self-Expression: It's possible to be authentic, but if we don't express it, nothing happens. Learning to risk sharing our gifts is central to Action Mastery. During the 1996 Presidential campaign, most of us got to know Bob Dole as a somewhat tough and ill-at-ease candidate. Once he lost the election, it came as quite a surprise to many people to see the at-ease, humorous person that surfaced. On the "Late Night Show,"

Leaders must have the courage of self-expression to reveal their doubts and weaknesses in order to build strong, trusting, effective relationships.

—Rob Hawthorne

David Letterman acknowledged the dramatic shift, and Dole responded, "After 18 months, I can be myself again." Wouldn't it be interesting to know what would have happened if he had risked expressing and being himself throughout his campaign? As leaders, how often do we lose our real power as we play to an audience instead of authentically expressing who we really are?

Leonard Sweet wrote, "The future is not something we enter; it is something we create." As leaders, we create the future through action. Sometimes we self-express through our mere presence, but most often it is because we take the risk and do something. We may end up disappointed if we fail, but if we don't take the risk, failure is certain. Most leaders we've coached over the years are action-oriented people. However, most leaders need to work on two crucial elements to express themselves more effectively:

1. *Broadening the range of self-expression we will risk:* Most leaders will be action-oriented over a narrow range of comfortable actions. For instance, one leader may risk getting things done but avoid the risk of emotional intimacy. Another may build relationships but not risk tough decisions. Often, the personal fears generating qualities of persona need to be dealt with to free up more qualities of character and a broader range of self-expression.

Challenge yourself to go beyond your comfort limits by asking, "How could I bring more of myself to this situation?"

2. Deepening an understanding of the inner dynamics supporting our outer actions: Many leaders will express themselves, but without purpose. Sometimes the compulsive tendency to act can reflect a fear to be ourselves or a fear to connect with others.

Challenge yourself to go to a deeper level by asking, "Is my action arising from my purpose and character, or is it just a coping mechanism, a persona reaction, to a situation?"

3. Action Mastery Principle Three: Creating Value: Many leaders get results; fewer leaders create value. Getting results is not enough. We can get results and leave a wake of bodies in our path; we can get results and destroy the environment.

INSIGHTS • REFLECTIONS • COMMITMENTS •

The altar of results is huge—we can potentially sacrifice everything on it. Unfortunately, many leaders unknowingly sacrifice their health, their purpose, their relationships, their lifestyle—all on the altar of results.

Creating value involves broadening our range of interest. It takes the limited, self-interested focus on results and expands it to the principle of reciprocity. Creating value seeks to reconcile self-interest with the common interest. In a dynamic, complex world this can be an extremely difficult challenge. Leaders must deal with so many conflicting constituencies: shareholders, employees, the community, the environment, and so on. It is difficult, but if we are going to lead from the inside out, we need to consider shifting our focus from short-term, self-interested perspectives to longer-term, common interest perspectives. Creating value versus achieving results requires that we ask ourselves in every moment of leadership, "Are we enriching life, or are we depleting life?" The closer we come to enriching our employees, our community, our environment, the more value we are potentially creating. Creating value forces us as leaders to move from the "What" questions which focus on external results to the "Why" questions which focus us on purpose and enriching life.

You must do the thing you think you cannot do.

—Eleanor Roosevelt

Challenge yourself as you are making crucial decisions to honestly reflect, "Am I enriching life or depleting life? Am I opening up possibilities or shutting them down?"

THE TWO STEPS TO ACTION MASTERY

Action Mastery is 75 percent preparation and 25 percent performance. It's like training for an athletic event. We invest weeks on end in the training phase. The more effectively we focus on the *process* of building our endurance, flexibility, strength, coordination, and mental focus, the more effective our performance will be. Just like an athlete, we need to "go into training" to strengthen our inner resources relating to self-knowledge, purpose, relationships, balance, being, and change. If we build our inner excellence, success will be experienced in both the process and in the results. Socrates clearly understood this inside-out dynamic: "Wealth does not bring about excellence, but excellence brings about wealth and all other public and private blessings to men."

What can you do to go "into training" to lead from within? Start with these Action Mastery steps:

1. Action Mastery Step One: Outline Your Growth Commitments. Review the growth commitments you made at the end of each chapter. If possible, lay them out in front of you. Look for the ones most crucial to your growth as a whole person. Look for recurring themes. Identify five key growth commitments you genuinely want to work on. Write down your key growth commitments:

1._____

2._____

3._____

4._____

5._____

2. Action Mastery Step Two: Build Your Awareness and Act on Your Growth Commitments. A core principle of our coaching at *LeaderSource* and the *Executive to Leader Institute* is: *Build awareness first, change behavior second.* It's an inside-out process. Programs focused on changing behavior first have some value, but it is more of a charm school, outside-in process. Under stress, most of the old behaviors return unless an ongoing state of awareness can be integrated into our lives on a consistent basis. The one-on-one coaching process is an exceptional way to build personalized practices to maintain self-awareness across a wide range of life situations. These coaching practices can be radically different from person to person. One of the unfortunate limitations of a book is that I can't jump out of the page and sit down with you to help design various ways to ensure your ongoing, self-generated progress.

INSIGHTS • REFLECTIONS • COMMITMENTS •

In lieu of jumping out of the book (wouldn't you be surprised), I have selected one effective technique for building and maintaining your personal awareness around your growth commitments: journaling. If you don't like to write, have no fear. Journaling is *not* about writing the great American novel. It is about building a practice for reflecting, observing oneself, and taking action. Your sentence structure and grammar are unimportant. It is a process for thinking, feeling, and capturing the essence of what is going on.

To find yourself, think for yourself.

—Socrates

The journaling process we have designed combines your growth commitments with the three principles of Action Mastery: *Authenticity*, *Self-Expression*, and *Creating Value*. Let's look at how this can work.

Don, a veteran marketing executive, was known for taking on daunting projects. He loved the challenge, and his track record proved that he was a tenacious builder who got results. When Don started his coaching with us, he had spent more than a year rebuilding the declining market for the snack division of a major corporation. Although the company's president appreciated the bottom-line results, he was concerned about what appeared to be Don's "super-hero style." The president wanted to improve profit in this division, but he also wanted a broad-based foundation of talent contributing to it. He did not want the results to depend on any one individual.

At our first coaching session, Don openly admitted that he always felt he needed to do everything himself. He was afraid of relying on others, yet he resented having to shoulder all the responsibility. After talking to him further, we learned that he felt this way in all arenas of his life and always had believed that it was expected of him to accomplish everything on his own. Depending on anyone, he believed, was a weakness. Sometimes Don was friendly and genuinely interested in others. However, other times resentment made him moody and unapproachable. He could fly off the handle at people for no reason at all. We learned that co-workers and family members were wary of his unpredictable behavior, and they were hesitant to ask for advice or to offer suggestions.

Clearly, Don needed to work on his interpersonal relationships and synergy. One of his leadership growth commitments looked like this: "To promote synergy in my organization, as well as in other areas of my life." When Don started to think about how he was going to do this, we guided him using the three principles of leadership defined in this book. We suggested that he ask himself: "How can I be more authentic? How can I deepen and broaden my self-expression in this aspect of my life? How can I create more value?" To address these questions, Don focused on some specific actions he could take, and he wrote those down:

- I am going to be more open to other people's style of doing things, and I am going to show this by getting feedback daily.

- I will meet with people at work to become more open to other ways of initiating and implementing projects.

INSIGHTS • REFLECTIONS • COMMITMENTS •

- I am going to give fair consideration to the ideas of other people. Whenever possible, I am going to encourage others to try out their ideas by giving them freedom to accomplish them in their own way.

- At home and in other personal relationships, I will ask for help and respect others.

- I am going to be open to other ways of getting things done.

- I will begin to work on this commitment by _____. I will keep track of my work on this commitment by journaling at least two times per week.

- I will have achieved noticeable progress in this area based on feedback from my wife, children, friends, and co-workers by _____.

Don realized that he needed to apply his new learning and activity in his business as well as in his personal life. Although he knew it would be difficult, he understood that if he could trust others, accept different operating styles, and let go of his shadow belief that everything depended on him, he would no longer feel isolated, resentful, and weary. He could focus his energy on developing his own talents and the gifts of others. His family, friends, and business associates would become more open and relaxed around him as he showed them that he was authentically interested in them and that he valued their way of doing things. As he learned to value others, they would feel valued, too, and that feeling would translate into more effectiveness as a leader, as well as better morale, mutual respect, and synergy.

The realization of the self is only possible if one is productive, if one can give birth to one's own potentialities.

—Goethe

Don wrote all five of his top growth commitments in his journal. Then he read them aloud into a tape recorder. He wrote about his reactions, his fears, and his hopes. Then he took the leap of sharing the commitment about synergy and interpersonal relationships with his wife and a trusted colleague. After these two meetings, we suggested that Don write in his journal all of his thoughts about those meetings. We suggested that he write about his feelings first, then about their reactions and any information he learned. As Don continued the journaling process, he felt less anxiety, and the people he met with did, too. We recommended that Don use his journal to make self-observations, to note what works and what doesn't. Don learned to be more tuned into effective ways of interacting. When an interaction did not go well, he thought and wrote about what he could have done for the next opportunity. This practice of writing his observations, reading and getting feedback, and then writing his thoughts again helped Don see himself more consciously. As he trusted that he could be honest, he began to lead from character.

LEADERSHIP FROM THE INSIDE OUT JOURNAL

We have developed a step-by-step process to help you lay a foundation for ensuring your continued self-awareness and growth. After you read through it, turn to page 197 to see a sample from Don's journal.

1. Designate a notebook for journaling about your growth commitments. You may want to set up a file in your computer if that is a more comfortable writing tool for you.

INSIGHTS • REFLECTIONS • COMMITMENTS •

2. Schedule time on your calendar for working on your growth commitments using this practice. Just as you make an appointment for lunch or a golf game, schedule journaling into your agenda. How much time? If you are thinking that you don't have time to add one more activity, honestly ask yourself, "What are the career and life consequences if I don't make this commitment?" Consider spending an hour at the beginning of the week and an hour at the end. If you are eager, you may want to spend more time, especially as you begin to see progress.

3. Select one of the five growth commitments you listed on page 187 and write it in your journal. Try to choose the one that you view as your highest priority. You may even want to work on more than one at a time, since often one commitment impacts another and it is difficult to separate them completely.

4. Keep in mind how the supporting principles of Action Mastery—Authenticity, Self-Expression, and Creating Value—

impact this growth commitment. Write these questions in your journal and reflect on them:

- How can I be more authentic in this area?
- How can I deepen and broaden my self-expression in this aspect of my life?
- How can I create more value in this area?

You must be the change you wish to see in the world.

—Mahatma Mohandas Gandhi

5. Be broad and be specific when capturing your responses to the questions. Beginning with the first question in step 4, write your thoughts, the *first thoughts,* that come to your mind. If you have difficulty continuing your train of thought, write the question again. You can do this again and again to open your mind and to build awareness about your authenticity. If you are having difficulty thinking of ways you can be more authentic, reflect on the opposite. Write about ways that you have *not* been authentic. This process will reveal the other side, and ideas will surface.

As you write about this growth commitment, you will have a variety of thoughts. Try not to edit them or shut any out. Write your *first thoughts,* the ones that immediately come to your mind. If you do, *your voice* will be the one you hear. Write them all down as they come to you. Some will be expansive and general; others will be focused and specific. To guide more specific thinking, ask yourself:

- Why is this an area I need to work on?
- What are the obstacles?
- What resources do I need?
- How is this commitment going to show up?
- When will it show up?
- How is it going to be measured?

Write each of these questions, then write your responses in your journal. Include specific details as much as possible. You can generate your own progress by targeting dates and making certain that you stay on track.

As you implement your ideas, listen to feedback, and trust your authentic Self, you will be able to measure your own progress as you clarify your commitments and reinforce your convictions. In fact, you can expect to experience a full range of emotions, from creative tension from knowing you need to work on specific areas to exciting breakthroughs from heightening your awareness.

6. *Read your journal aloud to go deeper and to gain insight.* Read what you wrote exactly as it appears on the page into the tape recorder; then play it so that you can hear it. While reading aloud you will hear your words and become aware in a way that is different from when you are writing. Did you hear anything that surprised you? Write your reaction in your journal.

INSIGHTS • REFLECTIONS
• COMMITMENTS •

Although you may think that reading aloud is unnecessary and you may be inclined to eliminate this step, it is an important part of the process. Being mindful as you read aloud is an excellent method of self-observation. It can help you to open up. It also prepares you to take the risk of going to someone close to you for feedback. Being open with someone close then prepares you to go to a broader range of people. All three steps will help you to deepen your understanding and broaden your range of self-expression.

7. *Ask one or two people you are close to—a spouse, a coach, a trusted friend—for feedback using something like the following process.*

- Ask this person if he or she will give you feedback on an issue that is important to you. Schedule a time and make sure there are no interruptions.

- At your meeting, ask this individual to listen intently but not to comment until you are finished sharing all you have written.

- Share your growth commitments.

- Ask your listener to respond openly to your ideas. Let him or her know that you welcome the person's suggestions and appreciate his or her reactions. For example, you might say, "Knowing me, do you think I am on target with commitments that will positively impact me as a person and as a leader?" Referencing a specific growth commitment, you might ask, "What are your suggestions for moving forward in this area?"

Take any step toward our destiny through creative action. . . . The universe turns towards us, realizing we are here, alive, and about to make our mark.

—David Whyte

- Now it is time for you to be an authentic listener. Listen intently and take notes. Notice how you are feeling while getting this feedback. Are you comfortable and open, or are your muscles tense and you feel closed?

- Take time immediately after this meeting to write in your journal.

8. Now go to a broader range of people you trust. Using the same procedure you used when you shared your growth commitments with people close to you, share your growth commitments now with a wider range of people. Ask questions and give them permission to be open and honest; listen intently. As you are listening, pay attention to your mental, emotional, or physical cues. If you have a strong reaction in your body, attend to that. When you write in your journal next, acknowledge this reaction and describe it as specifically as you can.

9. Write in your journal about the feedback you receive from others. Ask yourself the following questions to help you expand your thoughts and write about them.

- How open and receptive was I to this feedback when I received it?
- How open and receptive am I to this feedback now?
- How does this feedback broaden my perspective?

- How do I have a deeper understanding of this issue?
- What did I learn?
- How can this information help me implement this growth commitment?

Now return to the three core principles of *Leadership from the Inside Out.*

- How authentic am I as a leader?
- How deep and broad is my self-expression?
- How much value am I creating?

Write about how developing this growth commitment will impact your leadership in these areas. Use a wide lens and permit yourself to envision the positive influence of your growth as a person and as a leader.

INSIGHTS • REFLECTIONS • COMMITMENTS •

10. Take action. Formulate a plan that acknowledges your new learning and helps you to achieve your growth commitment. Continue the journaling process to increase your level of awareness through self-observation. This is an effective technique for monitoring your growth and progress. When you feel you have mastered one growth commitment, write about that and move on to another.

11. Continue using the journaling practice to work on all your growth commitments and as a technique that helps you on the pathway of Action Mastery. You are the only one who can bring your vision and voice to the surface so that you can grow as a person and as a leader. The more openly you write and listen, the more true your inner voice will become. The more you listen to your inner voice, the more you will lead guided by character rather than by persona. As you develop more self-awareness, your leadership will be characterized by the principles of Action Mastery—Authenticity, Self-Expression and Creating Value. This practice is designed to help you listen to *your voice*, to elevate *your awareness,* and to clarify *your vision*—the crucial components to *Leadership from the Inside Out.*

Destiny is not a matter of chance, it is a matter of choice; it is not a thing to be waited for, it is a thing to be achieved.

—William Jennings Bryan

LEADERSHIP FROM THE INSIDE OUT JOURNAL

— A "Sample" Page from Don's Journal —

Growth Commitment: To promote synergy in my organization, as well as in other areas of my life.

• How can I be more authentic?

• How can I deepen and broaden my self-expression in this aspect of my life?

• How can I create more value?

May 7

At the product development meeting, Karen made the presentation for Twirlies. Although questions were directed at her, I fielded them or interrupted her. I could have listened more patiently before expressing myself. I could have relied on her thorough preparation and competence. I'll try that next week. I will also talk to Karen and share my desire to grow in this area.

In the staff meeting I listened to everyone's project status reports. After each one, I asked, "Is there anything I can do to help?" I made affirming comments as appropriate, and at the end of the meeting I acknowledged the group for their great work. Morale was high.

I asked Bill to have lunch with me so I could get his feedback on the long-term marketing plan for Sweetbursts.

My son asked me to teach him about financial investments tonight. I proposed that he invest his savings in XYZ stock, and I promised to guarantee the investment. When he said he'd like to think about it and discuss it with a stock broker, I was angry. I talked to my wife about it. She helped me see that he was asking me to teach him how to invest, not do it for him. I could have given him a good book on investing, then offered to discuss it with him. I'll acknowledge my inappropriate response and discuss it with him tomorrow.

SEVEN POINTS OF AWARENESS FOR LEADING AS A WHOLE PERSON

As you work to activate your leadership potential from the inside out, keep the following points in mind:

1. Seek the Most Essential First: The core theme underlying Action Mastery is the principle of seeking the most essential first. Successful action begins with going deeply into our purpose and being. If we start here, then everything else will be taken care of. Besides, what is the value of success if we lose our self in the process? If we begin by capturing the fort, then the entire territory will be ours. If we spend all our time absorbed in trying to find a gold mine here or a silver vein there, then our "territory" may never be secured. But if we capture the fort (connect with ourselves at our deepest level), then the territory (our true success) will be ensured. If you're uncertain where to begin, then begin with *yourself.* You are the creator of your life.

INSIGHTS • REFLECTIONS
• COMMITMENTS •

2. Approach Growth and Development as an Integrated, Lifelong Process: Hoping to improve our lives, we often treat the symptoms of our behavior. For example, we want to be a more effective communicator so we master the "Ten Tips of Effective Speaking." We want to be healthier so we stop smoking, and so forth. Although these actions are certainly helpful and health giving, they only deal with the superficial behavior. When placed under sufficient stress we may return immediately to our old patterns. We need to be honest with ourselves: Are we just changing our external behaviors, or are we dealing with our growth on a more fundamental level?

Approaching our growth on a holistic level allows us to think of our development as a process versus an event. We grow as organisms. As we give ourselves nutrition on a fundamental level, all parts of our life are enriched. Realizing that our growth is organic versus mechanistic allows us to greatly accelerate our development. Going to the latest, greatest seminar may give us some interesting intellectual content to impact some aspects of our lives. Although filling our container of knowledge is important, comprehending the container is more crucial. Getting one profound insight can change our personal, professional, and spiritual life in one deep stroke. Dedicate yourself to personal awakening leading to transformation instead of focusing on process leading to change.

In thinking, keep to the simple. In conflict, be fair and generous. In leading, try not to control. In work, do what you enjoy. In family life, be completely present.

—Lao Tzu

3. *Take Total Responsibility:* Attempting to achieve success or fulfillment from the outside-in means that we have learned *not* to accept responsibility for our lives. The external world must fulfill us. The outer circumstances define us and our success. There is no true personal responsibility in outside-in success. Either we are created by or victimized by our external circumstances. Inside-out success is a total paradigm shift. We are totally responsible for our lives. We accept responsibility for our inner satisfaction and our outer circumstances. We are responsible for the life we have created, and we are responsible for how we deal with every situation that crosses our path. An amazing thing happens when we totally comprehend our personal responsibility: There is no one else to blame—for anything. You are it. There is no one "out there" to rescue you. Certainly there are life preservers of wisdom left by those who have gone before us. Others may be there to teach us to walk, but we must learn to run by ourselves.

4. *Value Consistency Over Intensity: Leadership from the Inside Out* works; but you have to work it—consistently—every day. Be careful not to rush into this with unbridled energy and enthusiasm only to crash a month later. Warm up to it. Do a few things each day. Integrate it into your routine. Start by focusing on one or two growth commitments. Involve a couple of people in your process for feedback and support.

You don't have to sprint to your destination—if you do, you may never make it. Walk through the great times, walk through the difficult times—just keep walking. Even small steps, supported by inner awareness and vision, will get you to your destination.

5. *Set Aside Worry, Doubts, and Negativity:* What are we doing when we worry? We are rehearsing our failure, over and over again. It is estimated that the "conversation" inside our heads occurs at a rate of 1,000 words per minute.

Since our normal speech rate is 200 words per minute, that's the information equivalent of having five people talking to us at the same time. Worrying is like having five negative, pushy people trying to convince us that things are not going to work out. If you allow these conversations to continue, you will "succeed" in achieving this negative vision. We have enough stress in life without unnecessarily adding to it. Set aside worry and replace it with "five new people" supporting your authentic vision and purpose. As Seneca wrote, "A man who suffers before it is necessary, suffers more than is necessary."

INSIGHTS • REFLECTIONS • COMMITMENTS •

The only person who can sabotage your success is you. You know, deep within, that you have gifts to express. You know your life could be more. You know you have dreams you would like to achieve. Doubt your doubts and nurture your dreams. Live the words of Franklin Roosevelt: "The only limits of our realization of tomorrow will be our doubts of today."

6. *Don't Just Walk the Talk, <u>Become</u> the Talk:* *Leadership from the Inside Out* is not about mastering a bunch of quick tips that will instantly change your life. Learning to merely talk about leading from within can become another layer of externalizing the real you. Intellectualization of our growth can enclose our potentiality within the boundaries of the process itself. But this is not the next flavor of the month. *Leadership from the Inside Out* is about consistent, integrated, lifelong growth. We don't master it by only understanding it. We master it by becoming it and doing it.

"Come to the edge," he said.
They said, "We are afraid."
"Come to the edge," he said.
They came. He pushed
them, . . . and they flew.

—Guillaume Appollinaire

7. ***Build Awareness Through Inside Out Journaling:*** Capturing our thoughts, insights, challenges, and inspirations is an important tool for having deep, reflective dialogue with ourselves. It can deepen our experience of growth. It can give us just the mirror we need to build awareness and congruence in our lives. The journaling process will allow you to have frank talks with yourself as well as to capture your progress and perceived obstacles or fears. Use journaling and other awareness-building exercises as a platform to awaken the endless levels of inner potential and outer achievement.

PARTING THOUGHTS FOR YOUR JOURNEY AHEAD

After years of coaching leaders behind closed doors, it has been both a challenge and a joy to take the time to share these principles with you. David Bohm once wrote, "The ability to perceive or think differently is more important than the knowledge gained." In this spirit, I hope this book has been more than just an interesting intellectual excursion that leads to a "smart book" gathering dust on a "smart bookcase." I hope it has been a thought-provoking journey for you. I also hope you have grown a little since you first opened the cover. But my real hope is that over time you will make the commitment to integrate the key principles shared and breathe them into your life. I hope each day you will take slightly "deeper breaths" until the inspiration is fully yours.

A few years ago, after spending significant and inspirational time with a teacher and mentor of mine, his simple parting thought to me was, "Bring peace, fulfillment, and awakening to the world." These inspired, purposeful words have guided me for years. So my parting wish for you is similar: "Bring peace, fulfillment, and awakening to all aspects of your life."

THE JOURNEY CONTINUES

A few months have passed since I finished writing this book. As it is with most things, "being away" for a while can bring a fresh, objective perspective. Reflecting on the book, I started to think, "What is the *real* purpose of this book"—not just the words or concepts, but its true potential contribution? What value can it potentially serve?

Certainly the principal purpose of *Leadership from the Inside Out* is to give people tools for *personal* growth and transformation leading to *leadership* growth and transformation. But its true potential contribution is more than that. Its purpose is more than just helping a bunch of separate individuals to grow.

Imagine a critical mass of authentic leaders who express their gifts and create life-enriching value. Imagine an organization like that, or a community, or a family. Envisioning a better world seems less like an idealized fantasy when you think what a critical mass of authentic leaders could achieve. As you move forward, I challenge you not to get lost in your own growth—the purpose of your transformation is to radiate your gifts in the service of others. Growth is fulfilling as it touches and enriches the lives of others.

I was recently working with the CEO of a major company known for his exceptional visionary skills and performance results. Throughout his career he had always been ahead of the strategic curve. He had an innate sense for what was "next" long before his peers or competitors. His long track record of breakthrough product introductions and marketplace successes was testimony to his exceptional gifts.

In his coaching sessions we focused on continuing to leverage his strategic excellence while helping him find more balance in his life. After about six months of coaching, global marketplace conditions had dramatically shifted and his company found itself in an extremely vulnerable position. For the first time in his career, he had missed a major strategic initiative. He easily could have diverted blame to many other people. Fortunately he did not. He faced the troops and took full, ultimate responsibility for the strategic oversight. He asked everyone for their support in moving forward. His authenticity, emotional courage, and self-esteem were strong enough for him to take genuine responsibility. As you would expect, morale skyrocketed, corporate energy was refocused, and the company emerged even stronger.

The only way to discover the limits of the possible is to go beyond them into the impossible.

—Arthur C. Clarke

As powerful as one authentic leader can be for an organization, a critical mass of leaders growing from the inside out can greatly accelerate organizational progress. Recently, the chairman and CEO of a firm invited me out to breakfast to discuss a new coaching candidate. When I arrived at the restaurant, I was surprised to be greeted by the entire executive management team minus the coaching candidate. In our meeting, we focused on the "issues" of their fellow executive and how each member of the team perceived what he needed to improve. After listening to their concerns, I was confident that we could help the individual, but that was not the real issue. Expressing what I sensed was the actual organizational need, I challenged the team, "What are each of you doing to grow as leaders in order to grow your organization?" In spite of their extremely aggressive business plans, no one could respond to my question. Clarifying my question, I said, "We can help Fred, but the real organizational issue is not to improve Fred's performance. The real issue is: How are you preparing yourselves for success?"

Leaving the meeting, I felt that although I had isolated their real needs, I had likely lost a potential account. Two days later, however, the chairman and CEO called me and said, "We listened to your counsel and felt you were right on target. I would like to discuss how all the members of our senior team, including me, could engage in coaching along with Fred." Within four months, the entire senior team was deeply involved in coaching. A critical mass of individuals was now rapidly transforming the organization. The chairman was now ready to let go of the CEO responsibilities. Since the members of the senior team did not want the CEO job, an external search was initiated. Key members of the team began to transform their roles, and new positions were created that energized the company and addressed strategic issues. A common language about growth and transformation permeated the organization. A new culture, one that would support growth and transformation, was now on its way. Like this company, organizations that invest as proactively in people development as they do in business development will thrive in the coming millennium.

I hope you have enjoyed our walk together down these pathways to mastery. I also hope you will share your blessings with others—share them with your organization, with your customers, and with your loved ones. Together we can create a better world. Connect with your essence and purpose. Bring your gifts to the world.

Until one is committed there is hesitancy, the chance to draw back, always ineffectiveness. . . . Boldness has genius, power, and magic in it. Begin it now.

—Goethe

BIBLIOGRAPHY

The following books are a combined list of both resources
used and recommended reading:

Almaas, A. H. *The Point of Existence: Transformations of Narcissism in Self-Realization.* Berkeley, CA: Diamond Books, 1996.

Arrien, Angeles. *The Four-Fold Way: Walking the Paths of Warrior, Teacher, Healer and Visionary.* New York: HarperCollins, 1993.

Bennis, Warren and Burt Nanus. *Leaders: The Strategies for Taking Charge.* New York: Harper Business, 1985.

Bennis, Warren and Patricia Ward Biederman. *Organizing Genius: The Secrets of Creative Collaboration.* Reading, MA: Addison-Wesley, 1996.

Bennis, Warren. *On Becoming a Leader.* Reading, MA: Addison-Wesley, 1990.

Block, Peter. *Stewardship: Choosing Service Over Self-Interest.* San Francisco: Berrett-Koehler, 1996.

Bolman, Lee and Terrence E. Deal. *Leading with Soul: An Uncommon Journey of Spirit.* San Francisco: Jossey-Bass, 1994.

Branden, Nathaniel. *Six Pillars of Self-Esteem.* New York: Bantam Books, 1995.

Bridges, William. *Transitions: Making Sense of Life's Changes.* Reading, MA: Addison-Wesley, 1980.

Byron, Thomas. *Dhammapada: The Sayings of the Buddha.* Boston: Shambhala, 1976.

Cameron, Julia. *The Artist's Way.* New York: Putnam, 1995.

Campbell, Joseph. *The Power of Myth.* New York: Doubleday, 1988.

Cavanaugh, Joseph. *Respectfully, Joe Cavanaugh* [video]. St. Paul, MN: Kelley Productions and Twin Cities Public Television, 1994.

Cleary, Thomas. *Zen Lessons: The Art of Leadership*. Boston: Shambhala, 1990.

Covey, Stephen R. *The 7 Habits of Highly Effective People*. New York: Simon & Schuster, 1990.

DeFoore, Bill and John Renesch, editors. *The New Bottom Line: Bringing Heart and Soul to Business*. San Francisco: New Leaders Press, 1996.

Douillard, John. *Body, Mind & Sport: The Mind-Body Guide to Lifelong Fitness & Your Personal Best*. New York: Crown Publishing, 1995.

Dyer, Wayne. *Your Sacred Self*. New York: HarperCollins, 1995.

Einstein, Albert. *Einstein on Humanism: Collected Essays of Albert Einstein*. Secaucus, NJ: Carol Publishing, 1993.

Emerson, Ralph Waldo. *The Collected Works of Ralph Waldo Emerson*. Cambridge, MA: Belkoop, 1984.

Garfield, Charles. *Peak Performance*. New York: Warner Books, 1989.

Goethe, Johann Wolfgang von. *The Collected Works*. Princeton, NJ: Princeton University Press, 1994.

Goss, Tracy. *The Last Word on Power: Executive Re-Invention for Leaders Who Must Make the Impossible Happen*. New York: Bantam Doubleday Dell, 1996.

Greenleaf, Robert K. *Servant Leadership: A Journey into the Nature of Legitimate Power and Greatness*. Mahwah, NJ: Paulist Press, 1977.

Hawley, John A. *Reawakening the Spirit in Work*. New York: Simon & Schuster, 1995.

Hayward, Susan. *A Guide for the Advanced Soul: A Book of Insight*. Avalon, Australia In-Tune Books, 1986.

Heider, Joseph. *Tao of Leadership*. New York: Bantam Books, 1986.

Hendricks, C. Gay and Kathlyn. *Centering and the Art of Intimacy Handbook*. New York: Simon & Schuster, 1993.

Hendricks, Gay and Kate Lundeman. *The Corporate Mystic: A Guidebook for Visionaries with Their Feet on the Ground*. New York: Bantam Books, 1996.

Hillman, James. *The Soul's Code: In Search of Character and Calling*. New York: Random House, 1996.

James, William. *The Varieties of Religious Experience*. New York: Random House, 1994.

Jaworski, Joseph. *Synchronicity: The Inner Path of Leadership*. San Francisco: Berrett-Koehler, 1996.

Jung, C. G. *Basic Writings of C. G. Jung*. New York: Random House, 1993.

Kets DeVries, Manfred. *Leaders, Fools and Imposters: Essays on the Psychology of Leadership*. San Francisco: Jossey-Bass, 1993.

Lowen, Alexander. *Narcissism: Denial of the True Self*. New York: Collier Books, 1995.

Maharishi Mahesh Yogi. *Bhagavad-Gita: A New Translation and Commentary*. Fairfield, CA: Age of Enlightenment Press, 1967.

Maslow, Abraham. *Toward a Psychology of Being*. New York: Van Nostrand-Rheinhold, 1968.

Melrose, Ken. *Making the Grass Greener on Your Side*. San Francisco: Berrett-Koehler, 1995.

Merton, Thomas. *No Man Is an Island*. New York: Walker, 1986.

Merton, Thomas. *The Way of Chuang Tzu*. Boston: Shambhala, 1992.

Morris, Tom. *True Success: A New Philosophy of Excellence*. New York: Putnam, 1994.

Offner, Rose. *Journal to the Soul: The Art of Sacred Journal Keeping*. Salt Lake City, UT: Gibbs-Smith Publisher, 1996.

Orsborn, Carol. *Inner Excellence: Spiritual Principles of Life Driven Businesses*. San Rafael, CA: New World Library, 1992.

O'Neil, John. *Success and Your Shadow*. Boulder, CO: Sounds True Audio, 1995.

Parry, Danaan. *Warriors of the Heart*. Bainbridge Island, WA: Earthstewards Network, 1997.

Patnaude, Jeff. *Leading from the Maze: A Personal Pathway to Leadership*. Berkeley, CA: Ten Speed Press, 1996.

Progaff, Ira. *At a Journal Workshop: Writing to Access the Power of the Unconscious and Evoke Creative Ability*. New York: Putnam, 1992.

Rechtschaffen, Stephan. *Time Shifting: Creating More Time to Enjoy Your Life*. New York: Doubleday Currency, 1996.

Satir, Virginia. *Your Many Faces*. Berkeley, CA: Celestial Arts, 1995.

Schiller, David. *The Zen Companion*. New York: Workman Publishing, 1994.

Segal, Jeanne. *Raising Your Emotional Intelligence: A Practical Guide*. New York: Henry Holt, 1997.

Senge, Peter M. *The Fifth Discipline: The Art and Practice of the Learning Organization*. New York: Doubleday Currency, 1994.

Shipka, Barbara. *Leadership in a Challenging World: A Sacred Journey*. Boston: Butterworth-Heinemann, 1997.

Suzuki, D. T. *Essays in Zen Buddhism*. New York: Grove/Atlantic, 1989.

Teilhard De Chardin, Pierre. *The Phenomenon of Man*. San Bernardino, CA: Bongo Press, 1994.

Tzu, Lao. *Tao Te Ching of Lao Tzu*. New York: St. Martin's Press, 1996.

Whyte, David. *The Heart Aroused: Poetry and the Preservation of the Soul in Corporate America*. New York: Doubleday Currency, 1994.

Wilbur, Ken. *No Boundary*. Boston: Shambhala, 1979.

Index

ABOUT THE AUTHOR

Kevin Cashman is Founder and CEO of LeaderSource, an international leadership and executive coaching consultancy. From LeaderSource's headquarters in Minneapolis, he has spent nearly 20 years enhancing the growth and effectiveness of executives and organizations. He is known as an expert in the design and implementation of comprehensive leadership and career coaching programs to meaningfully engage the talent of organizations. Some of his clients include General Mills, 3M, Novartis, Northrop Grumman, Medtronic, The Limited and Honey Well.

He has written three books on leadership and career development as well as numerous articles for national business and human development publications. He and his firm have been featured in the *Wall Street Journal, Strategy and Leadership, Chief Executive, Human Resource Executive, San Francisco Examiner, Fast Company,* and other national media. A contributing editor to *Executive Excellence* magazine, he was recently featured with Warren Bennis, Stephen R. Covey, and Peter Senge in Ken Shelton's book, *A New Paradigm of Leadership.* His new book, *Awakening the Leader Within,* is published by John Wiley & Sons, Inc. A frequent keynote speaker at conferences and corporate events, Kevin was formerly the co-host of the "CareerTalk" radio program. He has been a Chapter President, Board Member, and Fellow of the International Association of Career Management Professionals.

Prior to LeaderSource, he was Regional Director of an international human development organization and Vice President of a vocational services organization. His educational background includes a degree in psychology from St. John's University. A believer in dynamic life balance, he has participated in more than 50 triathlons and has practiced and taught meditation over the past three decades. He lives in the Minneapolis area surrounded by a lush woods, abundant deer, and a few very inquisitive foxes.

ABOUT LEADERSOURCE

*LeaderSource is a leadership and executive coaching
consultancy serving as a catalyst in the transformation of
leaders and organizations.*

Headquartered in Minneapolis, LeaderSource serves the needs of executives and organizations nationally and internationally. Some of LeaderSource's clients include General Mills, 3M, Novartis, Northrop Gumman, Medtronic, The Limited and Honey Well.

Offering an entire continuum of leadership development programs, LeaderSource seeks to awaken leadership at all levels of organizations and at all stages of career and life development. Key offerings in the LeaderSource continuum include: *Executive to Leader Institute*[SM], an intensive, interdisciplinary, one-on-one coaching program for senior executives; *LeaderCatalyst*[SM], a group-learning experience to develop high-potential leaders and senior teams; and *NewLeader*[SM], a selection and development process for senior level pre-employment or succession planning. For more information, contact:

LeaderSource
One Financial Plaza
120 South 6th Street
Suite 2600
Minneapolis, MN 55402
phone: (612) 375-9277
fax: (612) 334-5727
website: www.leadersource.com